- Journey through a Soul -

*

Verse

- 1982 -

Book 1

*

TRAUMEAR

*

*

– For those who know how to behave
in the presence of the poetic spirit. –

*

As human beings we develop and evolve. Poets have
the gift to make this intelligible. By means of verse a
poet can give us a running commentary of his own
growth and to the extent that he lives among us his
work, in this genre, can ease our own passage through
the contemporary doldrums. Verse can be a handy
technique for explaining reality in terms of experience.
Those who accept the poet's gift will find the present
work helpful in that direction and to that end.

*

1

My friend and brother, master too, great
teacher of teachers, met face to face here
by one who alters course and shifts opinion
but never strays far from his given task:

I look around me, awestruck and puzzled
perhaps by so much finality, and turn
once more to you whose image no more hides
the freighted person, dispensing such glory.

*

2

I have been set down, against my will,
(but since acquiesced) in a place most strange
where the earth and the sky seemed familiar once
until I scratched them, then the environment
became indescribable and I was frightened.

Today I manage to ride this happiness
mostly without a rein. I find that both times,
then and now, go into this single day,
my task being to show how they do it.

Today I manage to ride this happiness
mostly without a rein. I find that both times,
then and now, go into this single day,
my task being to show how they do it.

*

3

I call one thing the light of day, real clarity;
years ago, when I was not any more but still young,
flailing in a foolishness of sorts, I imagined that
merely this was required: to tear the popular
mask off the face of divinity, or, which amounts
to the same, to prove that a person could

stand defenceless before the charging hordes of
reality. Well, that done, the mask down, the
proof in the pocket, no one but myself believed.

Now, I suppose, comes the time for trapping
the king out in rags, for tolerating the several
supine adherents to the similar creed, since

only the very few can stomach authority.
To reach out into black space and capture
sensational treasure, tender, modest and mild,

by nature forgiving, of a habit merciful:
that's the thing. Save me from your stars, they're
in it irrevocably for their own light, while
desirous of death as the glittering evil at the same time.

Let me struggle with ease.

*

4

Spring drips well-being all over the environment again
and Jesus! I don't know whether to scream or to sleep.

I have noticed that a walk out into fresh air at this
time of year draws strange veils down and it takes
thorns of recuperation to get back into saddle.

Then, in a square room (bear with me) opposed and
confronted by indifferent demons, teenaged to show
how the present day contains all manner of metaphor,

my genius breaks out, begins to tear paper, scratch
walls, (hear the echo there) and plays the spirit vandal:

all eager to appease the sexual flair
that's thick and numerous in the air –

plucks handfuls out of human hair,
drives future generations to despair

and this to prove that nothing greater there
exists than boundless human care.

*

5

Care and despair both end in one
harsh sound like bed of thorns, yet each
commends the other, becomes it, depending
on will to do, on willingness to reach

gladly beyond the squandering heart
to start transcending, by suffering or achieved
crisis, peaks of compassionate art,
building hard sense where Isis grieved.

There's not a single trick under the sun
if it made the grade, from Heraclitus to Einstein
that cannot come into its own today,
and help us out in a pinch.

*

6

An age gave birth to me and died.
Often I pondered this occurrence when
justice grimaced at me from beneath
schoolbooks and the truth looked
willingly the other way while pain
between pleasures had its way with me.

The age of empires, called the modern age
closed up shop and moved to spheres unknown.

*

7

The interregnum between kings and the king,
no easy transition by any stretch of the imagination, because the common terms mean

living death and dead life intermingled (I
wish I could say it more plainly): this interregnum keeps us hopping. For myself I can

say it drives me round the bend. Television
breaks up time and shortens hours. Nerves
try to cope with simultaneous opposites, but

how can the grand gesture thrive while gossip
holds sway over values organic? Exports of
weapons to Syria, Cuba and Lebanon, or

guerrillas trapped on hills in El Salvador,
these expectations we take for granted, must
amuse or the pain in my stomach means

nothing. Revolutions are bad. Revolutions
are good. Anne Hathaway's cottage, burgled,
deprived of oak table and chairs, weeps in

the driving rain. I cannot be expected always
to make the connections. They make themselves.
All I can do is gently tend in the right direction.

*

8

Fatigue pushes me towards the earth's centre.
I find it impossible to shape a single thought
and yet I mean to continue, bullying and
shoving, squeezing through fog like cotton.

I mean this to be my life, and it may take
words like these to bank the aberrant stream.

*

9

For twenty minutes I watched how a
policeman tracked and eventually caught
a rapist. Ate peanut butter and honey
on brown toast, drank tea. I have

the choice to withdraw from this to a
quiet corner somewhere in this small house
but I mean this to be my life, to admit
whatever desires to come in. I have

my hand against my head, legs crossed
under a pine table, a thorn in my finger
from a bramble runner I severed today
and tossed on the fire. Oh, I have

a degree of uncompetitiveness to consider,
conclusions to draw, efficiencies to work
out, in the short term. A housefly crawls,
sits on the page's margin. I have

yet another opportunity, it would seem, to
legislate against my lazy nature, my slack
intelligence, my disinclination to fervour
in or out of court. Therefore I have

a case against the age from which my birth
stems like an echo, and its music drifts
like Elgar's mythic loneliness, like bitter
aroma from the viol, suggesting suicide.

No age follows the Modern Age
and yet men long to earn a living wage.
The Modern Age has ground to a halt
while institutions, worked up into a rage,
seek leaders, strong men, then collapse.

The pessimist, the morbid sage,
confuses tender care with traps
and hops on one leg to confound
the public gaze, the rigged progress report
and then returns to beer and sport.

* *

10

Weakness threatens to overwhelm me one final time.
The sexual spur digs in, draws blood. Incredible,
the circus here tonight! Tolerate, wait – abstain.
Be field, be crop. Be harvesting machine,
belts, augurs, wheels – let the seed come clean.

*

11

Where I go no man who knows not love
may follow. My eyes straightforward look there,
embrace the great variety of life
never to end, never to end, but jubilant.

What a change, that this should be so, after
two score years, when the cannon stopped
the mouths of children standing by my cradle
and flames blew from cathedral spires.

Where I go no mad thing may
lay snares for the conquering spirit,
free from revenge, from mercenary gain,
from the vile encrustations of citified life.

But if the cold should bite, the food supply
run marginal, I'd lie and cheat my way,
with honest face, through upper class estates
and raid their cupboards, with approval.

I know myself now, and my friend's mettle.
They've never set their softened faces sufficiently
against his ways to really risk his wrath,
so let someone film them – – .

Sure I began like the rest, but then discovered
myself prior to my beginning. I shot
holes through the timescale, bent back
death against birth and bore both away

into the distance immeasurable, right
here in front of my nose, so that the teeming
miles counted more than numbers told
or waiting warranted, in a lifetime.

*

9

What was, I ask, I then before the clock
decided to expropriate my life?
Prior to my birth I must have been because
my rebirth set me back before time was.

Son of man, earth spirit, contained
material me, to be turned inside out.
The stuff that went unrecognized by most –
a teacher once said: that one might be human –
lay dormant in the shell I called my self,
at which some pointed. Some refused to point
but glanced in my direction from afar
and mumbled nonsense. When I touched my skin
I thought I felt a dog's pelt and shrank back
into my flesh, reluctant, son of man.

I'll be what I am *then*, before I was,
and brook no interruption to my cause.
I'll start where that Italian brother left off,
peace in one will with him who holds us both,
determined to make parabolic flights.

An exile from the world of striving men
striving to exile more, in exile satisfied,
German a mother – English the father tongue,
forced by whatever nameless circumstance
to give up name and rank, and then to know
the value of that high, superior stroke –

that fate and choice become one flowering shrub
set by the roadside.

Call me that ruffian from the heart of Europe.
I would have had me different, don't you know,
but since we must, along with our own idiocies,
carry those of our forefathers, we might as well
desire to do so, and make an end of it.

I can recall the first ideal that plagued me:
genteel society and true conversation.
I've dropped a few ideals like that since then.
'That abject crew' has multiplied and thrived
these last two thousand years – this generation –

it matters what you call them: they react.
I never thanked the stone that broke my fall
when one time, in the north of England, climbing,
I looped the rope around some prominence,
rappelled the cliff down, slipped out of the rope
and windmilled downward.

The ability to pull thoughts from mid-air
stands in good stead him who advances care.
But angels have a way of intercession
that gets confused by many with depression,
a bad thing, inconvenient for our feeling.

The sense poetic finds such things appealing.
It takes their part, assumes to know what matters
and brews concoctions from the clouds it scatters.

It came to me one day – I still abhor
the memory of the pain – what brain is for.

For centuries plans have been in the making up there
waiting to be implemented. Others like myself said:

Everything has to be reworked. Everything will end up
totally different, but look the same. – We got together.

The suspicion that we were not going to be
hugged for our efforts encouraged us to remain obscure.

The most ridiculous assumptions (I still blush)
had at least to be entertained for the time being, since
one saw no way forward except via the total acceptance
pushed to the periphery, or answered simply in terms of
the person you were talking to.

The newness of this approach bowled many of us over.

But it continued to approach. You and I met and
turned into pronouns. Effective states gobbled up our
awareness of ourselves as human beings, influential
complexes swept our insistence on individuality under
the mat. We were not too happy about that.
One morning I got up out of bed and discovered
nothing but the distinct impossibility of finding myself.

I can be cool about it now, but at the time I trembled.
My teeth chattered. The perspiration collected on my
forehead. Well, not to get too dramatic about it,
I expected I had gone mad. The neighbours came round
and said words like: Hello. Lovely day today. And
I don't recall what I grunted by way of reply.

One feared that no reply at all might trigger an
attack of normality, and normality gleamed like a whetted
edge. I sit here writing this down and find myself going
hot and cold all over. Well-meaning relatives telephoned
the experts. I must confess that one by one the
professionals arrived. The attention did me good.

Their intentions made me think fast.
Lines have never been
invented, learned and delivered so quick and in
one go. My heart skipped all over the place.

Let me tell you, I write this down now out of the purest concern,
for those who like me would prefer to make sense of everything.

I can well afford to go back to that icy spot in the attic
because now I'm equipped, inured to the white spirit of Athens.

Time has taught me how to abstain in comfort under rafters
where Tom stemmed parental reproach and moved to the tower.

The classic drift from naked meadows earns only my trust now
and I thrust contempt under the noses of those who would see me hang.

Enough. The flame that burned here once,
a tongue with appetite for destruction,
turns downward now, in inward glow
and there, akin more to the hearth,
provides the heat to forge my name.

* *

13

As I get older I learn the value of trust on principle.
So much of my past rises periodically and furnishes me
with pleasure and nutriment. The rash promises of youth
are replaced by solid gains. My conduct improves, especially
in effectiveness and I still devote most of my time to love.

Unhappiness does not frighten me so much any more.
I accept that the development of new life within me takes pains
and I try to carry these burdens gladly. Poetry helps
immensely when it comes to suffering confusion. Strength too
responds to it in my case and those who use it come to their senses.

I want to achieve a more responsible seriousness in my work.
This means dispensing with the provocative remark for its own sake
but I must allow myself to be affected by my own weaknesses too.
The invention of techniques for success against spoiled parts of my nature
depends on the depth and compassion of my experience in their light.

Take this cursed readiness to flare up in anger for example.
But my heart goes out to those who love by accident
and they weary themselves, each other, driving out soft demons.
Meanwhile the wood darkens and all the deer are slaughtered
or the moon rises where dead men weep to be so misguided.

*

14

I am alone in all this like others,
attempting to make grief recognizable.
It contains the appraised word still
but threatens to bury beneath blind fear
patience and the willingness to love.

A nest hangs lopsided among wet twigs.
A fox looks up, sniffs and passes.
The rain starts again, gently weighing down
broad leaves, jagged from the frost,
and the meadow grows green and dark.

Never say love dies, for love is action,
not like happiness, coming as it pleases.
Even the feeling of love is up to us,
not accident, its absence to be feared.
All things are given into our hands.

Sometimes I confuse the result to my activity,
such as high spirits or a profound humour,
with the fundamental situation of life,
as though man could rely on his kind
or cause his mate to behave wisely.

The organ booms in the cathedral nave,
the bass draws darkness from the walls
and roars to fill the spinning vault
while stained glass takes sweetness from the light
and injects it into eye and heart.

*

As soon as I have stopped loving
I suspect that I am on trial
and viciously justify myself.
Sometimes loving is not like pushing
a button located in space and time.
As circumstances change
so does the technique of love
and its starting place moves.
For example I may be outraged by
an injustice perpetrated against me
by someone whose person I do not respect.
I shall most certainly have to improvise.
Basically however, in my case,
to love means to wish to love,
an entirely scientific strategy.
I have made it a fairly secure habit
to regard love as the cure for all ailments
and as the solution to every problem.
I gained this habit due to much thought
and application during the last twenty years.
Due to my particular vocation I do not
live confined by degrees of positive and negative
character, which would, I suppose, permit
corresponding degrees of self knowledge,
but the potential depth of my depravity
is unlimited, just so as the potential
magnitude of my virtue and bliss.
In either direction no finality exists and
nothing in my nature guarantees a point of fixity.

Angels, bad or good, are liable to visit me
at any time of the day or night.
My work could in no way be defined by
an eight hour day, or described in terms
of a forty hour week. I have no holiday
as such. My vigilant attendance is not
regulated by the clock but tied to eternal
life.

Obedience to god in my case means a speedy response
to a lessening in my wellbeing, to a depletion of
my joy, to a shaking of my certainty, to an under-
mining of my comfort, to a darkening of my happiness.
I do not mean to imply that obedience is everything
but it is part of the work that leads out to humanity.
Responsibility to god is the same as responsibility to man.
Only from a position of non-involvement in either,
chained to the split oak or perched on the ice floe,
does it seem that the one is two and that neither is whole.

* *

Change

This is a time of total change
where even time makes gentle swing
towards claims of love to entertain
  everyone and everything.

No right of passage or routine
of transfer lets our soul ride high
unless, by some ambition sore
  we labour love – it passes by.

Trajectories of remembered life
are worked out and appeal to men
who live elsewhere, some other time,
  not eased of this bleak 'now and then'.

Our actions pass through hell and world
but only to make tracks and flee
and then, cleansed of such travel dust
  as clings, your love returns to me.

And who you are all men may know
whose heart has entered in this sphere
and whose belongings, kept in trust,
  unkindly to the eye appear.

*

17

Unless I now and again do work that
enwraps me completely in truth I become ill.
As soon as I make my senses available to
your particular wavelength, my friend, all
disease vanishes. Age takes its toll by
fitting the flesh as limit to greater
capacities, setting our sights for us.
A new pain signals a crossroad.
Some pain should not be moved but left
to move us and together we set out on new
roads to new places. The vexing pain
close to the heart makes new contacts.

Speech, where the heart or the head alone talk,
can easy do damage, by too much perfection.
Some brilliance blinds the untutored eye
and heedless warmth sets tongues wagging.

Love escapes from the routine trap –
a new moon failing to light an old sky –
as age is borne, on raised arms, through the portico
and laid to rest, to sleep with past misdeeds.

*

18

Only one illumination was required in my case.
I slipped from clutches refined by education.
A worthless life met me halfway down the
enlightened corridor. Beneath the window stood,
eyes gazing upward, grinning mouth transfixed,
the widowed bachelor, halfway house for vagrants
on their way to hell, as Dante described them.

There I recognized the great danger of lassitude
and for years afterwards the white demon beset me
as I lay dying. Oh fond relief from death
thus transmogrified! I mouth the sexual phrase
willingly, gladly allowing the tension to
subside, furthering in this manner
progress I'm not ashamed to recognize.

Some men have captured in their loins
the access route to those celestial plains
that, once achieved, make ideal claims
and must be entertained. A few go on
and choose to do what they must do
but these are the very few. Only one sowed
where I reap.

*

19

My life consists of world and truth,
the one I trust, the other I love.
Magic I hold not in esteem.
Whatever is but will not seem
let it remain obscure.
Rather the heart pure
than some semblance of worth
by greed and usury underpinned.

Let those who have not sinned
build their temples to righteousness
and to the propriety of decent minds.
I have no trouble with their kind.
A formal type of social skill
does not make world unsafe, nor kills
the small, gem-like being
that prefers looking to seeing.

The teacher wants out today
to walk among the people.
He classifies his hopes in terms of
food digested and money invested
but how he does this must be left to him.
We dare not interfere with every whim
brought on by passion or seclusion.
Our minds must suffer some confusion.

Whenever I refer direct
my heart to brain, not circumspect
by way of once experienced nature,
only the tiniest touch is required
and a new generation of offspring is sired.
Nothing new about that, except
they're not born for the block.
My children's home is built on rock.

Not sleep should be repeated
or the death in absolute strife
as though identity meant love
but the ever revolving application of body
or mind in growth towards the promised end
of life and more abundant life,
which growth in truth is rooted
and world gives shape.

How perfectly our language suits us
while we allow it truth and world
and eat its substance while we speak.
Or in this visual form of speech
our care may reach
beyond confines of space and time
in interest of variety and
in interest and variety we understand.

Don't bully words.
Trust that some less familiar link
may lead you outward from mind, to think
pleasures more closely, joys more near.
Who knows how nature should appear?
Are you, creator, not in your self free
to shift and change
and make new love, even absent-mindedly?

* * *

20

Shouldn't anyone be able to make
the trees grow, the wind blow?
I'm ashamed of these words leaving
my mouth unsung, unheard,
as though an ill wind blew them
across a dusty street.

The work I feel needs to be done
but my understanding bends both ways.
My mind tackles each successive problem
with new tools, with a fresh appeal to
this eager pleasure recently left with me.

But I do want to avoid the sodden fields.
An easy perception of love's labours
does not often coincide with a rational brain,
therefore I take our time here seriously
though without loosening the fetters too much,
in case the aged beast should rise again.

*

23

21

I am cooped up in death's environment
while outside the birds sweetly trill
and sunshine splashes over woods and meadows.

But I don't feel I would be right to complain.
After all, once death has done its necessary work
we'll all be out to sport with love again.

My concern for mankind's global health,
not being undermined by policies,
cannot conflict with a single person's love
but springs from the same committal care
lodged in all judicious hearts.

I make my peace with love at last –
at least that is how I would like it to be,
not to quarrel with the bitter taste in the mouth,
and when the soul goes dumb like stone,
numb like a limb unnerved –
I turn to you, tools in hand, not despising
the least offering, before the great deed tries.

*

22

Sometimes the ringless circus moves so close
that I throw my hands in the air – then it draws
me in too. Rubbish piles up before the eyes in
clouds, Must I prove like this, too, that
    nothing can hurt me? Some pain exists
for mysterious reasons, if only to connect,
like the spider's thread the web to the blade,
the felt love to a worthy object. Once a moment's

peace has been conquered, build there.
Ravenous mouths feed off plentiful crops in any case,
in the biting sun. An image creates an interlude
    for any man, whether he plucks his joy off familiar
relationships or dreams his time away on hot
beaches, provoking an absent fate. Make no promises
because the vile shapes readily attack each other.

It could not have been dealt with otherwise, this
streaming experience of an aged reality. It had to be
settled on the butcher's block. But give yourself
    no airs, friend of creation, son of worship.
If the circling vultures come down nearby, their
raucous voices leave your eardrums burning,
behave normally, quietly. Trim the wick on your

candle first thing in the morning. Respect the clouds
harbouring precious cargo. I trust the man who
leads his life in and out of tight corners, furnished
    with maps for all the earth's immense reaches
into and beyond a woman's most intimate heart.
It would strike fear into your own, to see so much
spoiled time strewn where natives once wandered

tremendously appraising each new move, sharpening
wits against cold skin, labouring in the surf.
There they caught perfection in coarse nets
    and prepared each day for the next day's
failure and disappointment, loath to cultivate
success only, but reacting to each small god
as though men counted and man were an abstraction.

I run no risks while these weird woodland creatures
haunt my sleep, or like cataracts off cliff faces,
sifted by wind, they protect themselves in my blood,
    too narrow to be missed. Where we stand
we listen to the appropriate sound, fixed to no
schedule of self-advertisement. What we need has
muscular appeal, and the achievement of it

feeds some, not millions. Therefore ecstasy, hence
the illumined bit, crossed by straitened circumstance
and fast living, ice floes, cracked. What has
    the love you practiced to do with this
faultless jungle, these ringless circus? I speak
of an altered mission, stone borne forward into
flesh proximity, the granite face, no barrier.

My life exudes the happiness of love, and
mixed into it the butterfly's mad flight
trembles along sightlines. No barbed affectation
    fools the mouse in its grassy hollow. No
flirtation with the one-hoofed worker of miracles
manages to set up signs that last and last.
To an altered mission I bring the original fervour.

Trumpets crowd out the lost souls' cries.
The yellow brass exterminates their eyes, though
terror still stalks, and will stalk, while death
    sets spectacles forward on sunburned nose
and kicks up his heals at such a deal.
Balding at his age, how he feels the eyes
of customers on ware, soft breasts, smooth loins!

Sunning myself on Whitehead Beach I mused
on marigolds and copper beech, while the curlew flew
winsome overhead. I fell in love that day
    with nervous Jill, and she with me,
but trouble tracked, like wheels, our love down
and once again the meadow breathes.

*

27

A ship sails suddenly into view.
In spite of this bitterness, my life may
again become bearable.

Above the lake the mist draws
the clouds down. An elk
wades into the shallows and drinks.

Oh will this downpour never stop?
Due to my passion I must learn
patience and the will to live.

A forest fire has razed the hillside.
Now the stars look down in pity.

They have ploughed the fields into extinction
and their settlements darken the landscape.
Who are these gnarled creatures?

Machines protect our leisure against
too much care for trivia,
but only while freedom informs our works.

The heavy snows of winter still lie piled
around my heart, my brain, my mind.
I wonder, will spring ever show up?

The grave is black and I avoid it;
not from choice, but because
my path leads elsewhere.

Church bells and bluebells ring.
The reason for so much jubilation
is strictly my desire for it.

*

24

The exactest of descriptions makes the elements fall
    into place.
I have energy for many when it comes to the mortification
    of evil habits.
The sun king has slipped and fallen into his
    pauper's grave.
While the restitution of universal values proceeds, I
    simply make love.

*

25

I see too many images of swords for my liking.
Perhaps, you may say, I sleep safely in my bed
because a thousand angels wake and protect me,
and somebody has to pay their salary, son! –

but down at the well the villagers gossip
while Alla Mil Vallée dances for the UN,
leading them in worship, rhythmic dance tunes
piped into hearing aids while the flesh throbs.

I worship the silence at the centre of my being,
descend there by stair, soft on plush carpet,
leaning on the shoulder of someone's mistress
and my brain ticks, ready to make music.

Go on, behave as though the sensuous life
had invented your pastimes, had strewn petals
onto beds of nails; building permission is granted,
you may set yourself up as doctor for the few.

*

29

Once more I have in my self overwhelmed
the barriers to reality and its person.
Some new love I was taught – how to return
and overtop – not shrink from it and squander
in weak disorder, in affairs of hearts.

I see this more clearly now
how a child may trust us
asking to be sweetened
and we do run some risk of corruption;
it sharpens our ability to respond.

I want to tie this experience down well,
lash it to the deck, that a lovely but firm,
gentle but wise response may be mine in future,
and perhaps in addition I shall reap
fidelity's reward, a faithful mistress.

Since my master has moved in with me
most visibly, and he gathers furniture:
an end-table, two chairs, a wardrobe,
make of these what you will – I welcome
with varying degrees of trepidation
all signs of change in myself, since change
cannot anymore but be of benefit to me,
whether glaciers separate from peaks or
gleaming ridges break the eyes' hold.

Here, not in mind's eye, is where he lives,
but introduces himself there. Here nothing
stops him, not the trout hooked under the
road bridge, knocked to make it still,

nor the classroom atmosphere, known to all,
where young men hope, young women gather,
    and dust collects on books on shelves
    before a thousand years retreat.

*

27

    Please do not hear me, but my voice,
and him therefore, who lives here, that
all may remain well, as he wills it who
    contains all even as once fulfilled, never
to be broken, as he broke willingly
    so that we may all praise and praised be.
        I crash into many houses,
        break doors down, intrude,
        all to create that one creative interlude

    that none may notice where the beehive stands,
    cultured embarrassment; or my nose

discovers between the scent of leaves
and fragrance of fair skin a certain

        I don't know what. I twist
        and turn to help the light persist,

31

and know these pages burn
with an impending glow
while my poor flesh rages
because it would not have it so.

Oh tiring truck with time! Wearisome
commencement and finality! Street
hewn into rock-slide-ridden slope,
(where only troll and goat may cope)!

Transition from the sad-eyed doe
to telling people what this means
while the dead rise,

though my flesh would not have it so
but otherwise.

Some form of madness on the optic nerve
presses distinctly. This is to slice
the psychosome from body-love.
I've done it once or twice.

The staircase down, the thermal draught
up along the cliff face – both mean one change.

Smoke cheats the fly, disseminates the mood;
for some, the greatest because the least, must
study their god, steady their gait, before

their heart admits their head has closed the door
and now the choice looks different, either
freedom in pain or in beauty – never neither.

This puzzled me, before I learned to count
on fingertips, this most astounding, most
astonishing fact among many others: namely,
that you are where we are by choice

and therefore I encourage those who would
be guarded at the moment's unimagined point
against all disappointment, great or small,

    that what we know
    builds or corrupts us all.

And while the mayfly dances
where the cypress creates a space for leisure

stupid evil squats in the cold yard
intent on bending metal.

*

Because I entertain no thoughts of love
but only what the great white northern storms
blow down to me, sweep through me and
leave me a shell of hopeful resuscitation,

I gently act the fool a while,
hop up and down in someone's kitchen garden,
flirt with that most egregious lot
of loafers tied to a
vanishing world's apron strings

and jest from both sides of the mouth.

Sometimes I risk a calculated guess
as to the half-truths thrown up all around me,
but mostly it's a case of first come first struck
and the pale sky takes the measure of my perfection.

I know you by the company you keep
and first of all these are my own companions
not heedless of the warning voice
slinging mud, enmired in the cabbage field,

but neither prone to vacant superstition,
praying to gods who measure things by size
or numbers, as if that could count.

I love you by the works you do, for my sake,
through me for others. Love means being accepted,
and you accept my being end to end.
This willed love always keeps me in the picture.

I educate through it my inner spheres
and make pronouncements, powerful enough
to move some mountains. Love is great
or small, depending upon the object or the subject.

Like a stream, dreaming itself forth through conceptual force
past active cliffs, beneath a cloud-gathering sky,

this power holds magic in its thrall, by implements
not known to the unwise. Death stalks the innocent

beginnings in us through the undergrowth, teaching
in gamesmanship survival, flushing from his lair

the bristly boar, red-eyed in blinking disbelief
that once again his controlled world should come to grief.

*

29

My heart has hardened and I beg
forgiveness for it. It should be otherwise.
I do what I think is best, and then,
like most, I have second thoughts,
even as I record them here.

Once our heart has hardened,
what can be done to improve matters?
First let me confirm my confidence in you.

I kept going, merely, and slept,
and that night much was explained to me,
though as yet I might not explain again.

Some action seems required of me –
and you might like to compare this to yourself –
such as a perseverance in line with truth
perhaps of an educational variety
and afterwards I wonder: have I done right?

I don't want to get caught up on this,
letting it become a fixation, or an obsession,
as frequently happened during my adolescence,
which I understand now, with hindsight,
as an untimely desire for roots where
no soil had been made available by experience
and probably the instinct for love was neglected.

Now I want to raise children which I call
'children of our own', meaning that I
hold myself responsible for the growth of
their spirit, and all else comes anyway.

Being a parent means learning from
history of the sort that has left tracks
in our hearts, connections in the brain.
I want to avoid making the same mistakes
but usually it's more difficult avoiding the
opposite mistake, arrived at in some
impatient rationality, some rationalized
impatience, so that the murder is not committed
but permitted, and the cruelty is not perpetrated
but allowed. I wish to be too certain
too soon, and I fear the tentative approach.

As spring comes, there is a new food supply.
The near dead limbs creak and decry the novelty.

But this is March, when tiny flames begin to lick
from the rosebush, otherwise of aged ugliness.

The chaffinch flashes white wing bars
on its way from the willow to the oak.

Thick glossy buds stick out on the horse chestnut,
so tall and grand, perplexing the sky.

Then the fascination for it suddenly runs out
and man is left with a plague of lethargy.
The previous season still calls halt to speed,
but in that dragged restraint my brain sees
the coming task: soon some new mouths to feed.

All themes and signs and rhymes would be rejected.
The truth means to step forward unprotected.

Do not ask where to love, but that you love.
It penetrates the chicanery of the seasons.
Of course some times god presses and obliges,
in which case only speak and sing. The burden
imposed, or not prevented from imposing,
is not a dumb thing, but willing to be used.

This is how I learn,
by turning myself into the loving pupil
and I maintain that anyone can do it,
though I have given up long ago

attempting to change wills by exhortation,
preaching the presence of a will towards good,
encouraging the cultivation of some intellect
in the name of a land or of its people –

the number of ideas is infinite
and let him who thirsts drink. My works
satisfy me first, and I know that I am a
human being, irrespective of my number.

In the very conception of work –
not games for fun, to pass the time, nor
self-imposed torture, to sacrifice individuality –

lies creation of self, which implies all else,

so that we do not need to add altruistic motives.
Of course the moral bosses soon point fingers
at the various abuses of self: self-gratification,
self-love, egotism and such, all of which

happen supposedly, I won't argue it.

But how does pointing fingers at them cure it?

Oh, I am a simpleton to mention it.
It should not be mentioned.

I've often been accused, by those who mean well,
that accuracy in kind ... I'll not go into it!

There's so much life about today
that this vessel is like to burst its seams.
Sunshine poured on the yellow pine table top
exemplifies it all: the small fire in the hearth,

and the flitting memory of another previous moment
much like this, when the host of hosts entered

and started speaking, to set things right finally.

* *

30

My condition is not the best.
Various illusions of illness plague me
and I would like to be able to say so.

In the factory the lights flash on and off.
The yellowish light reflects on lime green walls.
A stuffed eagle in the corner collects dust.

A certain degree of solidity is required
before we can communicate with each other.
Then it depends on the whiteness of the light.

*

I am not immune to the marching hordes,
not satisfied with stretching out in the sun,
so the meadow and the babbling brook force
no words from me, no admission of guilt.

I look up, and the cool morning's light
etches new thought in, sets me an example
of impartial gladness, never mind false men
or weak women, whose bodies negate love.

*

31

You may sit there
reminiscent of a higher awareness
wishing you might have power in life

    but the ideal content of your mind,
pressed against a background of appearances,
    demands its own rights,
    makes itself felt urgently.
    Therefore know that the power you seek
resides in the execution of good will

    and no man may overcome you there.

*

The struggle in favour of the five elements,
    sword in hand, book from mouth,
produces gladness over a still depth, and

often nocturnal spirits whisper in he air
    or transform themselves imaginatively
as the improbable budding of passion's rose.

*

32

I have arrived to become part of the lake at evening.
Here I do not wish to interfere with what surrounds me
but to drink in the eternal presence of all that lives.

It does not change, but only the pale light moves me
to consider with pleasure how far efforts have brought
me and those who trust me along this path to peace.

*

33

The day moves in a trance
along preordained lines of communication.
Those who do not believe that
anything is possible at any time
must daydream their way to fallible conclusions.

But in the reeds shivers
he child of the age gone by and it seeks
solace from clouds not descending, bearing gifts,
but passing overhead.

*

34

Water surrounds me in high waves
   and the moon performs acrobatics.
Branches of trees softly wave.
    No fruit there.

At the bottom of the well I look up.
    How did I get here?

The bill hook cuts off nettles by the roadside
   and the goat gnaws at its foot.

The men have broken sandstone from the quarry
   but will that fence hold there?
   And the hedge hiding the bird,
will it hold back god's hand from me?

*

35

My stars have underscored the sky.
An image folds back from the mind
and holds together for a minute

while the cows manoeuvre their bodies
through the gate.

The fox lifts his head.
I make no excuses for the fox
and while I question my beliefs
my pipe goes out.

What, have you noticed
how children become more brilliant?
They play the violin at birth
and juggle apples as they speak
to robots of a life at sea.

Do you wish you knew better?

*

The spider's net concedes the vision.
The dewdrops bring the light to bear.
The pressure of the brain's derision
sets heavens up and takes us there.

The boulders rush down slopes of mountains
and bury what the cities hold.
The lash comes down to strike the body
where life is neither hot nor cold.

A man may utilize destruction
to underpin his hopes for gain.
The final say lies with corruption
as truth makes every matter plain.

*

37

Five lines about love

Love is a horrid thing, I confess,
when mixed with tenderness
but unimpeded by mankind
and I find there is no redress

for love informed by wantonness.

*

Five lines of love

A narrow escape I had one day
when the world's vision sank away
beneath the great horizon round
but suddenly my poor life found
in you its ground and its main stay.

*

39

Ten lines celebrating the night

Through me these barren hours feel their way
and I have no care but only to survive
to end this business of unseemly dreams.

The vastness of the mounting chaos inside
lays low the spirits we have gathered up.
Their illuminations of the heart's round space
require the distant darkness of the night's life

and I lie down, showered by answered questions
all gathered up before the droll moon rose
to inspect this dreadful stage in man's affairs.

*

40

Sonnet
Celebrating the Light of Day

For me you mean what Greece has meant for some:
I mix in no nostalgia with your being.
Some hordes of men have fled before you come,
since love's meek ways must make room for your seeing.

God rides on your effects as on great clouds
as he makes known his final retribution.
If my heart's imperfection sometimes shrouds
your bright intent, this high-lit institution

of ideal man in man as one man's right,
I hold no image of god's love before you
but take you as you are, in all things quite
reflection's child, and no man may ignore you

whose future welfare meets with past tradition
in this ripe find: day's light by god's permission.

*

41

I would be healed of this:
the suspicion that I ignore usage.
Good bread pains me –
wine rises where the rash deed
leaves scars to remind the messenger.

I have contained my goal
and carried forth the hunt's ambition,
so long laughed out of countenance by
rude children in old men's clothing.
I desire no reward for it.

But keep me the moment's fitting sense,
and dreamscape where bold alteration
wrecks no law, no detailed,
experienced force through nettles.
I would sustain my argument.

God give me peace to reap.
I despair of illusion's ruin.
The mill grinds my flesh, and the storms
rage once again and trap me where
no lovely thing survives.

But the tendency to let life go
where it will runs deep with me and
I search within as though the sun's rays
met an obstacle where the oak
hides runes beneath gnarled bark.

*

Overcome this unwillingness to work
as though the remedy depended on people's opinion.

You might as well expect pain to
push you towards a solution as to
grasp at pleasure with bare hands.

So raise yourself up to a position of responsibility.
The globe may moulder or rust, the earth quake or
bloom in profusion, the world heave and sigh,

only what touches you is your business.

In cheerful modesty apply yourself
even to the worst evils that come you way.

*

Work for what? for whom?
For the world to remain endless?
To train the eye, see it is so?
What purpose behind this record,
this journal of spirit growth?

I wait and observe from silence.

*

Why do you hold my hand during this struggle?
Does it perhaps mean you have left?

I make no issue out of a rejection.
The whole point of a cataclysm would be
an immersion of the pain we espouse.

Therefore take hold of love and exaggerate,
if need be, all my most holy examples.

Probably we have the union of all
mankind in mind when we pretend to know
more about love than plants and beasts,

but our favourite pastime still remains
torture and absolution, as though
the probing mind found no fortune.

*

Be as far from the lax crowd
as the imposition of luck allows
and trust to no unwieldy fortune

since the day has an excitement of its own
trapped in the modesty of confusion
and we prefer an unlimited gain.

* * *

43

If you don't want to perform for the beasts
but you'd rather impose your presence on strangers,
    let it occur to you that you must die;
    such an idea has merit in it.

The institutions make room only for each other
and we concern ourselves with more subtle thought.

By a coincidence, the bird's rational appeal
magnifies my forgotten joys, in youth,
always on the verge of dropping down over crater rims,
    saturated by a sense of self –

*

44

Now the cat burgles the contents of my heart
    and the eagle picks my brains clean
but these are all intimations of puberty
and if I were to lie down under a sky full of vengeance
    some would still believe this and hold it against me.

So I act according to a more marvellous law.

We only meet when we keep each other fit.
Our classic experiences are shared by all
due to the rain that drops and the mist that rises,
and by the time the next crew arrives to man the ship

your wild fantasies will probably have mastered themselves.

*

45

And I have only toil here,
but the moment I look towards the sunflower,
whose open face puts me in mind of the world,
    I am again made peaceful.

    There's sanity in my past
much like bread in a basket over the shoulder,
or do you not suspect brilliance when it lies,
    father, and do you not hope?

    I bring gladness into hearts.
My gestures have an energy geared towards love
and the mild style of life here has an impulse
    hardly more able to quicken.

    I clearly identify my time
and stand observing beneath the crown of the
transformed sycamore, and the blackbird is
    mightier than man in song.

    So too each organism prays
according to its chemistry, in the soil wisely,
smartly in air, and so on, filled to burst
    with an immanence beyond captivity.

*

46

I sit on home-made stool
in my thought busy and careful,
much by love drawn
and my skill no end knows

but you to please.

We have done many things with ease,

together, apart
and ever our first art
changes and makes more fine
the dross of people's tongue

as here may appear.

So what great fortune holds
might sink or perhaps rise
in this gentle love steeped,
peace and rest ingathering

though few know
while others I dearly would invite.

Open or closed
these doors, my eyes, let in
vestige and manner pure
no man to tempt

nor sweet love to pre-empt.

*

Another World

Over the drowned hills rolls
another world, bequeathed
by love's two thousand years.

Read in the hence-pitched clouds
route and rude trek
towards outlying crown.

And though the still sly swallow flits
through minute aperture into bower

we may gladly crowd round
such love to inspect
as this world would reflect.

The harmonious church's reach
into willows by backwaters
where flows the Cam – oh shy

bleak beauty, now ageing
or winnowed fruit presaging –
cannot make force make cause

only the dull damned churls to entertain
or their foul sleep with blessing to imbue.

It well behooves me too
therefore to crack
some skull to bring truth back.

*

This world has much to recommend it
and let me say, as I see fit,
that those who grasp, to seize and hold,
    be it prestige, or land,
    or diverse riches,
in Israel, Ireland or the Argentines,

spoil themselves, their chances, and not
the world. The freedom they've got
they abuse. Let me do better.
    World knows no brink
    nor true triumph
and we compete but to make meet.

*

We should remember the force that tears
at what we build, demanding justice.

The energy that springs from deeds
and breaks out into light or flowers

is measured now. Sit tight and use
the world's ideal flame, not its name.

* * *

Hermes, not invincible, the flag bears,
   wind-drawn messenger and thief.
The brain searches for the bright analogy.
May the nation be advised as a person?

To neglect our conscience collectively makes
   worse sense even today than to
     perpetrate a stupidity myself.

The Falkland Island British population
   should be taken off to England now
and then should world opinion be persuaded
to press the Argentines to release
their hold on land not gained honourably.

The nation that acts hypocritically
and cares more about what people say
   than about the ability of its own response
must be brought back to sense by kindness.
The Prime Minister can ruin a nation easier
   than she can keep it secure.

Am I wrong to suggest how a political
leader should act and is this not my province
   or should every person apply some
aspect of the soul to the wisest management
   of the commonweal? Every person should.

*

49

How I set my feet down on earth
    in a while, one by one,
and someone with me walks a space
    making it less cumbersome,

this may surround you with some warmth
    or an altered mind secure,
bearing some question of these things,
    of a trust that is pure.

And I lower my sights for a time,
    not content with speed
but mindful of a world in love;
    on its fruit we feed.

For my heart, as I walk, creates
    wondrous things to see.
The steeple, many words, a buttercup,
    all these pertain to me.

But the cruelty in my heart breaks
    much I would see whole
or stops my path with stones of wrath
    as I walk towards my goal.

*

50

I am not angered by the past.
I would rather speak to the tribes than
rest with my eyes closed. And now
permanently abandoned within earshot
    of the coarse islands
I must take a stand on human life.

Why do they bend before a storm whose
meaning prevents all reflection?
Works leave us all gasping for air
and as I struggle against bad blood
    my head gains weight.
Clouds lie among trees, take root there.

Still, I wonder at my audacity.
Could any man be prepared while
a thousand insects claim sovereignty
instead of polishing their wings
    and locating characteristically
the bloated effigy of a midnight sky?

*

51

A wooden man, I collapse on the floor.
Too many sensations spur me on to love
    and night wind seeks my spine.
I have flattered the loose women until
    they take me for one of them.
    This is organized crime.

Lower down I swim in pools of anguish,
my feet trapped between broken staves.
    Would it be too much to ask
to have these animals removed for a century
    to let me get my breath
    and a degree of calmness back?

Silently the basket is lowered over the wall.
A few bleak stars locate the cold sky
    to explain this brittle feeling.
An older person slays me with his wisdom
    and the temporary clouds make
    room for the words I speak.

*

52

The shadow on the bindweed falls,
not on the crumbling sandstone walls:
– these words are graven on my brain.

I enter where the pain holds fast
and trees surround the burnt-out sky
for heaven's swan would fly at last.

I walked here when the flames drew forth
from empty ash an arduous dream.
These visions held me bound in spell:

The eagle with a man's head,
wings flowing light, so softly shed
on night sky, meaning love remembered –

the flight across dead earth,
skimming, attached to wood, over
bodies of rodents mangled in mud.

Chanticleer on the parapets
in triumph over history's success,
and the astonished, benighted population.

A figure enthroned in judgment,
fleshed in contemplation, oozing peace.

*

53

It hasn't occurred to us to drop Easter
    so the pattern belies its origin
        and the torchlight procession drones
           over the cliff.

Since one year makes little difference to another
    although we probably trap each other
        following the passion of song,
           our organism chides itself.

These personalized messages in make-belief
    frighten or illuminate, depending on
        the elements exorcised: how far
           we are willing to follow.

Naturally it would spare the world's feelings
    if we collaborated on this and
        took ourselves to task about
           ghosts and things,

but being fresh out of analysis and syndromes,
    our calculations go amiss if
        major forces are not taken
           forward into time.

*

54

I could say what others say,
simply flay my bones sore,
    organize for pay,
there, see that robot, it thinks,

and then across the ocean wide
take my flight, call it:
    a new world,
promises for the sexy ladies in bikinis.

But a fat lot the devil cares
for teeth not sharpened, for
    a creaky hinge,
set me down gently on fire, and

where I dig he digs, mixes
rubbish in, spoils for effect
    what I do, but
never folds up under the pressure.

*

55

Dada

I may suggest that pain
      nibbles at my heartstrings
or fits flowerpots into me.

I may pick at sky blossoms,
failure scrapes my skin down
    and I witness classical illusion.

By now my way is clear.
An imaginary performance has kept
    anguish at bay for a time
      so that the lantern

    stands bare, there,

    behind those people.
Or by another route these eggs are
flavoured by the frozen feeling
    elaborately stated.

On careful coalescing
the fishing boats migrate north,
    turn over,
and fit thimbles into place.

*

56

If you're in love,
　　love;
if you're in pain,
　　suffer:
use life as a buffer.

Daily doing makes
　　reality,
or else it breaks
　　mankind:
put to use what you find.

Absorb into flesh
　　pain;
urge growth to turn
　　eternal:
let be the infernal.

Work to make love
　　last;
take time to take
　　care:
soon we'll be there.

Now we've arrived
　　here;
keep to the world's
　　trust:
do what you must.

*

57

Is it not true that pain teaches me
    patience and tenderness?
Has the arrow not left the sinew before
    the path of flight clears?

And yet with the speed of light does love
    shorten my lifespan and
tall figures make their appearance here
    where the heart is moved.

*

58

I should not operate under the open sky.
My hood darkens my face and covers
    the self-infliction of an early age.

Apricots hang into the orchard's terrain,
full of the juice of a fearful love's
    temperate testament and flavour.

I can hear the crowd of malingering actors
trudging along the rails in mute obscurity,
    performing to make eyes red,

while an understanding is formed out there
as the world leans towards endless values,
    to accommodate the truth in person.

*

59

I meant to love
but her flesh confused me
    and the words she spoke
disinherited my mind.

I meant to love
and gave an account of myself
    but she only gazed at me
so I missed my opportunity.

I wonder, did she realize
that I meant to love
    but the powers I claimed
as my own did not please her?

Since she never loved me
    I have lost nothing,
so why do I sit here
    lost in contemplation?

What use is her image
    to me, who despises himself,
who asks: which comes first,
    the effect or the beginning?

Should I suffer or destroy
    by the way, who can tell me,
or does everything depend on
    whether I meant to love?

*

60

Did you suspect, my sweet violet,
that my heart was cold, not receptive
to secret glances, to chance contact with the hand,
that my fine mind needed to reject the rude gesture

and soon regret would haunt me, shame taunt me
for insisting on foolishness, pressing my disadvantage?

You waited timidly beneath the hedge of my obstruction
practicing insight.

The self you discovered to me gradually spoke plainly
of spring sun's gentle warmth diffused through leaves.
Why no one believes me when I make these utterances
and they stand back frightened, I shall never guess

for I know the clouded diffidence that prevents us
during the day from shielding our eyes' ignorance
while moods at night seduce us to violence.

What I call the heart makes allowance for courtship
and sexual tenderness stirs mine most successfully.

On all sides of me accidents happen
and I connect these up for your pleasure.

You would set up commissions in the wheat fields
under the songbirds' watchful eyes.

*

61

The loving relationship is prepared by the knowledge
that such a thing exists. The terrible snows
descend in any case, so adapt your heart.

In images lies the correct mode of behaviour.
You and I have set the sea to one side
and our eyes have met across dark rocks.

While the ministrations of the eagle to flight declare
how far our path goes straight before the next corner,
we introduce our personality to the naked light.

Why has the management of the world's affairs
become carefree inducement to black thought
while near these rocks the terns dive decisively?

*

62

I woke this morning not into love's kingdom
but strayed, and thought:
Where will my fortune lie? But speedily I repaired
to a nearby inn, where lodged, as I knew well,
an ancient friend, in these parts on business.

Should some description of the muddy road
and of the rain-dripping elms interrupt us here
or aid us smoothly, as did the cool fresh air me
across the village common? Crossed I one stile
or two? Blue mist lay shrouding our distant hills.

There stood the red brick edifice, the stone house,
walled and fenced round by privet, cypress and
black flames of yew. Remember, I had come to seek
advice, and so I strained to make my nature
small before the friend whose wisdom I respected.

I found him seated on a bench, watching
children at play in the yard. Suddenly I felt
burdened by the destiny I could share with no one.
He greeted me in a friendly enough manner, but
I blamed him for my failure to achieve happiness.

Afterwards I realized my mistake. Carelessly
I had come to question the world's wisdom, doing
battle with windmills –

*

63

Autosuggestion – dope –
no hope. No fun,
nearly on the run,
from ridicule, madmen.

I wish to be guided.
No principles arrive here
uninflated. The price
does not look nice.

*

64

A barroom brawl. Fifteen chairs broken.
An energetic reminder of a past life.
My brain threatens to discharge itself.

The heart makes contact. Realization
suddenly that at most the corner stone
shifts itself, though not for a reason.

Why should anyone appear in white?
A person begins to understand early
why voices from outer space mean nothing.

Then they have their comfort to consider,
the domestic giants, these gifted perverts,
perfectionists in the science of the will.

But you need energy again, did you know?
Peace eventually comes of its own accord.
We must request another look at the sea.

*

65

A caricature, sorely earned –
the heart, for years, has yearned
for eminence behind a mask –
ripe love in wooden cask.

*

Oh for the world's healing give,
for its healing give time; live
   to renew, to root and found:
once you live new, give ground.

   Anger stretches to surround
the imagined cage. Seek free
   access to the will concrete.
Set feet on iron age. Flee

   into heart's whole range.
You must feel strange,
   for strange kingdom's feel
unreal love makes real.

*

66

I speak of future events only with disgust.
   There are those who know love must
fail where time outdoes man's needs.
   Enchantment succeeds. The heart bleeds.

Contact with the wise makes matters worse.
   I neglect no remedy of course
but yield my will. Look how I yield
   meekly before your mild eyes appealed.

*

As a balloon will rise   by hot air lifted
or stones lie steadfast   by no force shifted,

this trust I bear   draws me or drives
much love from me   before love arrives.

Yet this still sound   trapped against my ear
some pity invokes   thin threads of fear

wound loosely round   this our boon
that we might love   and then love soon.

Have we hopes to rest   rest in glad truth
while some age gently   informs our youth?

By no means flattered   on account of tasted
beauty within you   nor yet wasted

through zealous deeds   I conquer my mood
and work employment   rework these crude

faction-insisting thoughts   to privilege linked
till mirror image shows   regress extinct

away from you children   from your tamed tongue
that no fair fitness   may remain unsung.

Therefore rule otherwise   love law if you must
slave of your selves know   our love loves trust.

*

68

Be still. Hold heaven's regard
foremost in turn. Retrace steps
pointed in perfection. Arduous

care takes the benign heart.
I follow the lettered traces,
make image twist scope to select

erstwhile cure in private places.
Engine spits fire. Warm heart
pines for illustrious message
but leaves cranium intact.

The Muse bestirs itself to act.
A contemplative raven rises
on thermal melancholy, leaves
bounds behind, moons enshrined.

*

69

I saw a man who used his hook
to cut the tall shoots from the briar.
He wore a grey hat on his head
   and in his heart burnt fire.

He stooped and from the clear brook drank
and rose again – and looked surprised
and in his eye some gentle shame
   my inward soul surmised.

He whispered, when I spoke to him,
that some would use his name in vain
and practice the poor devil's art
   to drive his mind insane.

I pointed to the brilliant sky
whence light so thick came that it lay
on winnowed grain in spilling blooms
   that quite took breath away.

But none of this assuaged his mood
and he returned to hook and briar.
He wore black boots as I recall
   and in his heart burnt fire.

*

70

Why can I not behave myself?
  I should never have come here
    to waste the time of god.

A crowd of people vexes the world
and liberty trains its own performers.

—

    You have time to decide.
    Open your eyes wide.
    Test the air with your tongue.
    Leave nothing unsung.

        * *

71

I have achieved a certain
   distance from my work
      because I slept

   and I kept
all my faculties alert.
I want you to understand that.

   Eat it in one bite.
   Take it down whole.
   Let it be of benefit.
   Penetrate to the heart of it
      in terms of digestion.

   Now ask a question:
Can we improve on the average day?
   Think about that.
Should we really risk
        the presence of our mind
   by forming an idea with it?

*

72

The impossible woman

If I could emulate some
other man's purpose, I would
soon direct his life too.
Let me infiltrate this thought with understanding.

A strange man knows whether I
care for him and how deep my
affection for his friendship runs.
By nightfall I would have him by love surrounded.

I know that other women
envy my position, so
intimately with him involved,

but they care not for the plague of injustice
visited upon the female sex striving
now for roots, now for recognition.

Therefore all cares accumulate in my heart.

But he chides my appearance,
leaves criticism on his dirty plate,
eggs me on to mere foolishness.

So I allow my passion out onto the hillside.

Then it stirs hatred up or
drowns his perfection in shame:
I am the impossible woman.

*

Woman's Interest

Your entire nature stands encased
in pride, looks down on worried minds.
But mine is made up, a feathered arrow
by love borne skyward, horizon –
then earthbound, truth searching out.

Like demons for masques ornamented
my plucked feelings slay one another.
Oh curious, this more than legitimate
betrayal of a woman's interests, when
no public interest minds her soul!

I grew to within a girl's length long
past noon of our culture, Sappho-inspired.
The tears trained tigers in me, my
unhappy affairs kept clowns in employment;
I planted these callow flowers, did you know?

Or I, gone on meadows to spring's end,
Lucifer trapped my virginity whole.
Since then all ways and by-roads ex-
clude the heart's restless direction in dark
performances, a hand placed over the mouth.

*

74

What have we organized ourselves to do?

The darkening shadow crashes to,
global warfare makes us pause.

Our leaders travel second class.

By the moon's diffused light we read
of images whose partial faces need
next to no trust to make them glow.

While our inherited children bleed
we say we want it so.

And so too, as the morning mist is driven
deep into the residual mind
where freeze the organs left to chance
rudely by a departing empire spirit,

an equal state prepares the host.

Such verities and edicts make us spin
in tribal conflict. We usher in
a hopeful age, unwelcome by most.

At current prices, who dares count the cost?
The teeming limpets cling to stone.
Salt moisture keeps their world apart.

Struggle to an amazing victory
and prepare to be bitterly disappointed.

*

75

A woman's tongue, a man's brain,
each drives the other one insane
unless by providence, or care,
they meet up with some power out there.

*

76

Our individuality should reach out
    and disturb itself.
How far shall it reach out?

Until reality presses in upon it.

    Then it gives in to reality and
    allows it to disturb itself.

Hold your heart out into the storm,
    also into quiet, sunny weather.

Always that which cannot be broken
    is broken up and that which
will not break, is broken.

Under the linden sapling we sported.

*

77

Your individuality is given you
  as a tool, not to lay waste,
    the elements do that in their time,
but to repair the wing of a collared dove.

*

78

Also what I call me at times rages,
utters the deadly cry, hates interference,
  does not welcome
a spade slicing into rich brown earth.

*

79

I am torn down, wrecked
  dismal under stones.
The eagle will not leave his nest.
The peak, unwarmed by sun, crumbles.

*

80

Look through the grass in seed,
  the scythe approaches.
  A hare sprints under the hedge
and a storm howls in the west.

*

81

All is not lost
but the magnificent light
pinpoints exciting times.

Look, in the garden,
last vestiges of spring
assembled there beneath the lime

or the tufts on the ash twigs
promise unfolding simplicity.

A carrion crow hops
listlessly through dried grass.
The train rushes past.

For all our errors we have
not much to show. Our plans
fit within silent settlements of

the flesh against spirit.
An aspect of our love
improves the mind's predicament

and arduous, the glowing sky
assembles there above the lime.

*

The mind has cancelled out the dust
impinging upon ordered light:

Formerly we drove bargains here,
steeped our souls in dreams and stuff
to placate anxieties derived from culture:

    a classic image might have suited,
    a point of order mooted –

Then strode, perplexed-perplexing,
that wide-eyed person onto the market place.
Trees hearkened, awake in the vicinity.
A flurry of doves became quite still.

Some individuals shouted : Appeasement!
Others, bereaved of the commonplace,

    struck poses statuesque
    and looked grotesque,

little aware of how this fulfilled the law
and that their hatred removed love's objection.

The true course of figured thrust
causes no pain, but pleasure.

*

83

I have this free time
   ahead of me, behind me,
     called life.

Clouds darken my visage
   as if to seem in themselves
   but they lay down burdens
     in my heart
     called life.

Tender zones of interference glow
   through to my skin.
An impaired vision accepts
   the black thing called bird.

So too this taste of rest decides for me
true love's injunction, and I remain
perfected, given over to eternity.

*

84

Not to invite anyone into this garden
but to tend the berries, to nurse the vine,
and then to give freely to all who desire.

Not to seduce anyone into this garden
but to step forth content in the knowledge
that much of value takes care of itself.

*

85

Weakness, come succour me, bring
pressure to bear on my love
and take in those words, those green hills
filled to surmounting with joy –

or can one man part such cloud
without fear generating partial opinion,
an empty sphere, prim thoughts,
to spare the world the shock of survival?

I make an allowance for love if it
speaks angrily, or sits back on chair
not precisely aflame with recognition
of thought in the vital appearances of flesh

but cannot countenance, not on casual
acquaintance nor stripped of honour,
the 'beleaguered city' approach to
problems caused for the sake of problems.

Therefore set me out several plates of food
in case I die of quicksilver poisoning
and must rouse the neighbours, speechless
on account of these stones in my eyes.

*

Now come the curtains down
of darkness in several flesh
and my longing for affection
    is roused afresh.

Now speaks the worm in base
matter with forceful tongue,
not willing the tender claim
    somewhat unsung.

But I sing heroics impure while
you still apart stand, fettered
to the poor penitent figure, secure
    though unlettered.

My cloak, for the tired refrain's
reflection, leaves marks where hot
touch gave cause for mixed applause
    and some did not.

Woo me on seeded grass the
next maid whose jubilant sound
works magic, though in laughter
    makes me profound.

Now tip towards the high ear
all of the heaven's illumined bowl
and carry such friendly mind forth
    as renders whole.
Eternal life has always threaded
these criteria of satisfaction.

The child dethroned some birds
to make nature commit to memory.
    Later the abrupt root required
as yet unsung soil to tap.
    Today eternity threads this sphere
here as anywhere on God's map.

* *

87

Like a wishing well, my sweet,
    permanent, cloy with treat,
        or vanish from form.

That may cure, make escape
    from mountain lake
        or quintessential norm.

Then rousing dead men's bones
    we interview rational dream
        so no one may know.

*

88

I have dealt with crimes,
kept careful watch near the lake;
orderly schemes attracted me,
and yet I heard no new sound

such as of the beaver's tail –
thwack – against the outline,
ringing in common choir,
and yet I saw only space.

*

89

I have not made a chore of these
mad talent encounters with love
because look where you will you find
the nearest hour at hand the finest.

*

90

The hunter through the wet field strides
preoccupied with thoughts of home.
The mild-eyed doe observes him there
and draws on its desire to roam
    steadfast to stand.

The dark light, pressed by heavy cloud,
contains the hunter's image true
and moist leaves cool the doe's soft nose
informed by scent unknown to you,
    perfect to it.

For all our weakness and poor world
we still maintain strong links of love
with beings who absorb their realms
of suited light and then improve,
    working life out.

*

91

They lost their way along the coast
where the geese
and the fat women on bicycles
all fit into one mind.

*

92

If I made a mess of things
would anyone help me out?
Would the carousing stop
that props up morale,
the dalliance with sex?

A monkey wrecks
my success with the ladies.
My raids on pink flesh
leave ashes on the steps.
With trepidation I advance.

Seemingly unrelated to sun and flowers
    I sneak up on the cultural lions out there.
My heart beats furiously for several moments
    and then pretends to stop, playing possum.

Why don't the tourists entertain me while I wait?
    They have nothing on their plates, their stomachs
are so empty that it brings tears to my eyes.
    Anyway, I make allowances for the cultural lions.

*

93

I sleep to make my humour last
and wake to give my brain a blast
since otherwise I get downcast
    and nowhere fast.

Too much anxiety brings me out
in rashes. Too much nervous doubt
concerns the world, makes people shout:
    We need more clout!

*

94

    We went to the sea.
The illusion of the sea was strong,
pine tree trunks framing the approach to it.
    The tern plunged.
White feathers pearled off salt moisture.
Oyster catchers stood at attention.
    The sun warmed the rocks..
Crabs hid in cold pools under weed.
We appreciated the sea.

*

95

The sea lay calm today
and an affluence of red sails gathered.
The late warmth closed us in.

Down on the shingle children searched
for shells not yet broken by the surf.
Quietly we sat side by side.

*

96

And all the shimmering of the sea
appears to you to mean to me
no more than eyesight's daily light.

The winding road along the shore
by plum in white bloom overhung
invites the memories we explore.

The countless sails, horizon-bound,
perfect this vision in our eye
and place our souls on solid ground.

A haze of atmosphere on fire
so seemly makes exquisite lore
that I shall love this sea no more.

*

97

The sea means rest for those who spoil
for lack of continence and hope.
I left the sea when I was young
and from life's hardship since have wrung
immeasurable love. I cope

less crudely with the sea in here,
to conflict much accustomed now,
to storms that break my heart's hard hull
and render death of love less dull
while monsters sleep below. I plough

deep furrows in the ocean's bed
and sow the sea's own peace down there.
An angry moment may suffice
to spell my intellect in ice
and then I wait for aeons. I care

for sea and land with equal ease
and flourish where the two make fast
by some agreement of the stone
that neither one remains alone
but changes with the wind. I last.

*

98

On a high hill overlooking the town
a tower stands, remnant of a past
submerged in courtesies of tribes
not well accustomed to the arts

of warfare as we know them now.
I often climb up to that tower
and contemplate surrounding scenes:
the sea withdrawing from the Lough

revealing beds of sand and rock,
the ribbed cage of its utmost peace.
Ships standing in the distant haze,
drawing the gaze, returning the eye

to illusions not so far removed
from the heart's power to will and weigh
or quietly to break trust in itself.
The soft tops of the aged fields,

by hedge confined or by stone wall,
gladly support the trust I feel
in my father's unmistaking care
of the child for whom all this was made.

*

Write something.
Anything at all.
There is a need to turn
fear into truth.

Why do the corners of your mouth
pull down bitterly?
Does justice not appeal to you?

I fear the discussion of that which
distorts my heart, or trivializes
the glory I mistake for my own.

Perhaps if I concentrate on
the energy of love, the generation
of knowledge for the sake of beauty,

my argument will achieve greater conviction.
Does it not limit the late hour, that
the terror remains banned in the oak tree?

Look, I have no desire to take advantage of
cruel idols to keep my fences mended,
nor will fine sophistication aid me.

The trembling hand on my face
pleases, encumbered by satin, gratified
by the touch through mystic glass.

Now I cross the magnetic bridge
and he who has proposed the deadly struggle
makes the vine bloom to trap me.

Tenderly envisioned, this dream presupposes
a familiarity with the birds of the night
or sagacity plainly etched on skin.

Nervously I shift in my seat woven of
green sapling, pretending no one watches,
or isolated against the sky by a worm's mentality.

Have I not broken with the perfection-out-there mongers
whose mouths ape seclusion, form-fast,
and their bursting bellies belie their bones?

Now I must act in the ripeness of the oracle,
phlegmatically disguised, then the pain sits
less as an issue upon the striped chairs.

The cosmos permeates what I intentionally feel;
the dormouse climbs the flaking bark –
as an image it rests in happiness.

*

100

The plight of man transmits
to where the pain sits
flowering on the window ledge.

The tortured flight of gulls
narrowly marks the tranquil eye
within, before the storm lulls.

I sleep on earth's crust
pressed as abandonment of sky,
embarking upon a new lust.

Fear never, fear no such taste
as crowns perception seedlessly
and attacks needlessly

brain cells in harvest not implied.
Embrace the slender waist
and please, dance inside.

*

101

All hail to the cats with demon faces
and pockmarked souls – all hail!
Their transmigrations to other lands,
other characters, shall not fail.

I, by amusement moved, shift earth
and calculate the infringements of stars
by rote, thin fingers clamped down tight
on catgut, stroking out tunes of Mars.

*

102

And a sadness may nourish your thirst
upon meadows where primulas first flourish –
Oh cruise, though cold winds grind harsh sound
from old wounds, among tropic isles, my friend.

Pretend on Patmos stood the wellhead capped
while the sea lapped prophetic visions from the dunes
and my spirit lies down, lets ploughshare strip
from the masked body its miraculous exclamation.

*

103

Upon a foggy night
the dressmaker's soul
slips from its post
to keep a tryst.

*

104

Soon the god who finds me willing
props up with his fingers chilling
terrors crystallized for viewing,
for, my love, we need renewing.

*

105

I am a man-servant to the count.
His volcanic temper erupts here.
Should we not take greater care?
I believe his 'highness' welcomes fear.

*

The poet sits in space confined,
the cosmos darkens his escape.
The varnished table leaves his mind
empty to contemplate the ape

caged and fitted with a hood,
made ungainly by his moods.
To concentrate he carves in wood
from which the darker grain protrudes.

A knight in armour canters past
and neither poet nor ape leaves trace
on warrior's brain, in vain at last
entranced within romantic space.

Love, I am poet and ape and knight
and as this trinity I bring
my love to bear on all not quite
yet live beings held in mind's tight ring.

And I would ask to be believed
or trusted for my master's sake.
The joy his suffering has achieved
must grow or cause the heart such ache

as twists reality out of scope
and panders to sick nature's whim.
The Christ I know stands 'rayed in hope
with active strength in every limb.

But what does this mean, I am asked
by men who cannot help but grasp
hot idols in whose sun they basked
and lewdly to their bodies clasp?

How can an image stream with light
which light attacks the fibrous flesh
and breaks down all resistance quite
to concrete power established fresh?

Will magic play the tune no more
while guile and usury dance with glee?
Have we not bought our lives before,
wrought contracts between you and me?

The violet dares beneath the hedge
to bloom while March still blear-eyed roars.
Sly robin clears the window ledge
of crumbs our human hand outpours.

Wisely the savage in his den
protects himself against false friends.
The journalist insists his pen
improves the world before it ends.

My own fear is that half this house
will fall before the rest is built.
These carefree values I espouse
make careful use of blood once spilled.

I hold tradition in great awe
but sweetly winnow chaff from grain.
The image of god's face I saw
means we see not god's face in vain.

For I see god as he sees me
not hidden but in truth revealed
and hate my self and would be free
to love myself, of all hate healed.

Conceptual science still makes noise
inside my brain-box and I plead
for riddance from these outworn toys
whose fust obscures the love I need.

Some pious rattlings still prove crude
obliterance to the new-germed seed.
I want brute strength to be renewed;
kindness belies the love I need.

Against brute strength, that it may work,
pit elements in turmoil there.
Let tongue stay single but brain fork
as water in earth, fire in air.

Then know that sun makes daylight pure
and erstwhile rises in the west.
Air subjugates the green heart's cure
and gladly entertains us best.

Fire brings the senses down to earth
once abstract thought has cleared them out
and water makes experience worth
its salt for all life round about.

And lastly earth takes hold of love
and manages to give it roots.
To left and right, below, above –
add through – and harness strength of brutes.

Here stop a while and look around
as viewpoints open into spheres
eternal, and no end was found
to rule this world as it appears.

But only show, in various modes,
how that world feeds the world we mean
and though it burns up or explodes,
this serves to keep our conscience clean.

Learn ever more in ease and peace
to thrive on what our nature gives.
All mastered passions must release
their booty, that our beauty lives.

All perfect impulse, mood and state
cannot but raise our power in trust.
What pain our brain cannot equate
with hate must settle down as dust.

And drives too subtle for our felt
emotional appeal to life
such as desires not yet propelled
by causes for whose time we strive

relinquish, where our memory treats
each passing moment to concern,
their fire demonic, tonic feats
deserved observing, as we learn.

*

Here stands our effort, and success
assured, we let the ripe fruit drop.
Oh man of fame, whose name we bless,
your love has raised us to the top.

* * *

107

The depressions we suffer in patience
in future protect us
from bad neighbour's insults and glances.
Foul moods affect us
else our heart grows deaf and dumb.

The logic of endurance
appeals at times of rest
but build on it, construct it, brother.
You know yourself best
when you question me, none other.

*

108

I walked through tall grass on a day
when sun through high cloud peered.
A friend from years past came my way
whose worldly look I feared.

He spoke of contest and of strife,
his words depressed my heart.
He left content, to live his life,
I stayed, to work my art.

*

109

I sent a letter to a friend
to ask him for advice.
I thought my poems lacked something
while his were very nice.

He sent me back this kind reply:
You're right, your poems lack polish.
I tend to build new values with
the old ones I abolish.

*

110

Sunshine escapes me.
The tree-lined playground drapes me
in gentle soul's contentment gray
while children play,
and the thousand flames,
whispering now, performing here,
emanate from the trying times
shaped in stone and wood and glass.

Some curious wish drives me
to flatter the birds, the benign sky
crushed by falsehood in my brain,
permanent. The myriad stars,
imagined as in twice-filled eyes,
patterned to mask an angel's face,
make legal my desire, give proof
that no man remains aloof.

*

111

If I could bring myself   to rely on god's power
I would never hesitate   not in the least hour.
My illness would I stand   poor man's luck suffer,
never ever complain   because of god's power.
Sometimes I forget   my part in a planned world
and temper upsets me   so that I spoil my hour.
People inflict on me   the wounds of my weakness
while the universe turns   secure in god's power.
Strange fears seize me   I quake and tremble
and should watch carefully   through the dark hour
but harsh words betray me   words of my making
in bitterness spawned   as I flee from god's power.
Most of my failures   could well have been avoided
if I had spent more time   in dedication to the hour.
We may satisfy all desires   no matter how primitive
or wrought up in shame   in trust to god's power.
My leaning to falsehood   taste for cheap glory
hankering for might   were all poisoned in one hour.
Now I work every day   while daylight permits
or a bad time requires   to grow in god's power.

*

112

If we remain tranquil at times
and our love makes no new beginning,
how can we fail, denouncements aside,
to make no new beginning
there, granted we live
and stride into future events
blinded by too much excitement.

While the harsh fears hold
or tremble like leaves in wind,
fill sails with bright hope.
As easy exercise in love you may
hunt among tentative remains,
ten times more sensible now.

Look into casual eyes bleared
by magnified tears, haunted again
beyond endurance by the piecemeal
flesh in birth pangs unidentified.

We cannot make promises past laws,
none of us can, though some do, literally.
We cannot exorcise the worm, only
perfect ourselves, and leave our selves
open to the worm, to its ravaging
and crazed rampaging, and cloying
sweetness past bounds of taste

and then soon the intruder returns
and looks us squarely in the face
and makes no claim for reparation.

*

The Same in German

Ich bin müde, mein Leben
hängt wie am Faden,
zerbricht, zerschellt.

Mein Wimmern, Jammern
keinem Mensch
die Seele erhellt.

Trotz alter Weise
schleicht sich mein Denken
nächtelang weiter.

Mein Klagen, Leiden
stimmt keinen Mensch
froh noch heiter.

Tausend Stimmen schwirren
mir dauernd wie Falter
im Kopf herum.

Steinerne Wege –
Pfad durchs Gehege
kehrt nicht um.

Möcht zittern vor Freude,
allein mich hindert
der Menschen Gebrumm.

*

114

Bitterness, you're my familiar,
disappointment, be my friend.
The injustice I have suffered
brings my cowardice to an end.

The vexations of your spirit
have developed my care.
I look forward now to sunlight
and to healing clear air.

*

115

I come to you for help.
The fire burns me and
I fear the consumption of myself.

Around me summer smiles
while aged mourning
rages within.

She holds the world,
my love and her pride,
and relents slowly.

I must be prepared
though I praise your ways
and my freedom conquers.

*

116

Outside night darkens hills.
Yellow the streetlight fills
nothing where no one stands.

Moonlight on window sills
magnifies people's eyes
even as church bells ring.

Look, we have everything.
Doubtful, the penny drops.
Love me, the whole world stops.

*

117

Once again peace is with us.
I don't know how long it will stay.

You protect me where I go, if I
ask you to do so. We sneak

into no corners, past no fears.
My room reflects the settled state of
an eager mood. Longing is contained.

Here one may build, today,
at a time when protection suits all
manner of thing, and images arouse
their fill of desire. We look past

objects, into space, terrified,
meeting with no resistance. Imagine
how this would look on your grave:
Permanent fixture – son of man.

*

The Coffee Morning

Look how the ladies perch,
cups on careful laps;
some reclining in embarrassment
waiting to be chatted up
to where some ease would please them.

Enters the bear and pushes at tables.
'Sit there, we'll wait on you.'
Gently a slim hand touches the
nervous fur. 'Go on, sit there,
I'm here to make you comfortable.'

A cup appears, steaming black.
Baked goods bedeck the table top.
The varnished ceiling gleams,
sets off the white walls right smartly.
The bear risks a cherry tart.

Talk comes round. One feels,
opines too, makes observation.
The bear exclaims, leaves pause.
A vicar departs. His gray suit
casts shadows down the corridor.

What are coffee mornings for?
The bear reflects, rejects the judgement,
shifts to strike the required pose,
reaches where pockets once contained
silver and gold, a cheque book –

but sadly grumbles a remark
happily heard by no one.
The house and all contained therein
may suit the imagination of the bear.
I seems you too were there.

*

I am not altered by your state of
   wishful renown. I hear singing
deep in the throat still of the past
   and a sugared conversation would
change my outlook only if it meant
   an angry outburst at the end.

   It seems we have come at last
full circle, or as tradition would have it,
   to that plateau not parched by heat
nor yet made inaccessible by snow,
   and a thousand trembling requirements,
arranged along a social scale –

permit me to take heart, my friend.
   What, if we met now over tea,
or by some strange quirk of the imagination
   sipped Virgin's Milk, seated round the campfire –
would any part of music's memory
   the stars involve? the flesh absolve?

   Someone forgives stupidities and
I've worked my share into a bright world's
   sorrowful festivities. What only
language such as this may risk I risk
   or would fail in my duty as time's
chosen cardiographer, by pleasure blinded.

Could it be that you too sometimes
   feel free to overlook the pains inflicted
by growth's necessity, and range beyond,
   where boyhood seeds through the applauded
earth's crust tentatively germinate and
   pale green overflows the field?

*

120

Go again to the field
and stimulate the drum beat
or vex the wild beasts there
dressed in humanity

as open-eyed,
perfection not despising,
the doe lacerates the frozen ground
with cloven hoof.

*

121

Sigh these wind-still spaces shut.
Rely upon the gold of buttercup.
Serenade the tragedy of some love's
floating insecurity behind bars.

Disturb the clouds in Phaeton's cars.
May laughter keep you well hidden
from the poison thistle and dull friends.
You have my gentle absorption.

Yes, I am anxious for my soul's
fine operation on the moonlit beach.
Here we must strive to bend and reach.
Our clever devices leave us in the lurch.

*

The Cistercian Abbey

- 1193 –

In the cloister it occurred
that the visitor pretended
he stood among lively monks.
They chatted and joked,
made fun in their cassocks;
one rocked with laughter.
But they lived eight hundred years ago
and only the proximity of sympathetic warmth
brought them out into the open.

The visitor marched round the refectory
impressed by buttresses as the sign suggested.
There, the hatch into the kitchen, still preserved.
The day-stair: three steps, then open sky.
While monks sat, ate, one stood there, read,
above the rest, book in hand, in a niche,
a figurine most functional and appropriate,
reading, to keep the minds of eaters elevated.

The Pellitory of the wall grows
lovely green against soft sandstone,
curvilinear leaved stems seeking
sunshine, soon to bloom.
A blackbird shows anxiety near its
nest, a hole, bespattered, where the
blocks once met but water hollowed
the space between, where now
the fledglings screech or heed the warning call.
Children are told to stand still and observe.

The crowns of trees behind the ruined walls,
willow and yew, holm oak and sycamore,
have cought thine eye, oh contemplative visitor
and even through the high, high windows, like slits,
foliage pours in, with no respect for privacy.

Stream up, in vision, yonder chimneyed wall
and mark the outline, leave the cloud behind.
Perhaps a mystery draws your heart out like this,
that where you stand, by solid peace transfixed,
the air seems charmed, the light not quite contemporary.

> Grey Abbey, complex of ruins,
> mortared foundation walls,
> a bit of chaos nearby behind
> the wire fence, where lords-and-ladies
> yellow for lack of sun beneath the beeches –
> the rooks quarrel in your vicinity.

> This must be the breeding season for rooks.

> They'll not keep quiet, but they
> worry the air with their
> drifting and flapping.
> It costs a few pence to enter

> and the bespectacled warden in his hut
> counts out the change, tears off a ticket.
> One more visitor to swell the trade.
> Beside the path, behind a wall

> a puzzle mends itself while people
> strangely continue to proceed
> one foot in front of the other towards
> their particular reason for entering.

* * *

123

No ideas come to me, and yet
I sit in this cave of thought, surrounded
and hemmed in by popular destruction.

But lift, lift up the beam, take
fully into account the marvellous light's
grave challenge. It rushes

through crowns of ashes, disturbing
their massive equilibrium, yet
again they return to majesty.

And this my experience says to me:
Thou art small. Be thou still small.
Lift not thine head inopportunely.

Yes, I would not gainsay such advice.
The glowing bluebell desires no
auricular confession but traps

in its root all manner of impurity
so that the sun, herald of love,
may later in beauty transform itself.

*

124

I search outward in god's knowledge
for the token remnant of fire.
Here some weeds trail thick
to develop the limbs' strength.

Among that which looks worthy I see
the machined soul, lustrous gift,
heavy in weight, objective substance,
a polished eternal structure.

Meanwhile, if memory of our presence,
master, points out a sense impairment
such as the perfect individual content,
please judge the fool mildly.

I would practice, against this life,
my virtue in weakness, to gain
the only solid approval, and pain
stakes my claim in spirit.

*

125

Train me to cancel out ignorance
and the broad track towards the border
must suit the selfless man.

I submit to conventional bias
because my heart possesses all keys.

Where no beauty helps me up
I condemn the fabrications of death.

*

126

Why not instruments, pathos, to wreck
the tender sentiments of love's passage homewards?
Be gone, fervour before the mind's eye;
let fly the rational animal, beyond retrieving!

*

127

Teach me to observe the childish ways,
the warning light, not interest for its own sake
but the tender virtues of a crushed heart
resembling no fathomed truth, nor final divinity.

*

128

I am situated where no man believes
and my instant cognitions belie your life.
Therefore beware, fully estimate the value
of man's honest approach to the holy light.

*

129

The whole of my life has been one long start
of love conceived as an object of art
and yet with all my being I devise
death without effort and without surprise.

I want to give my life before I find
I have too much intelligence on my mind
and the error seated where my flesh collects
liberates the reality my brain expects.

Therefore I feel myself forward in thought
to invest the life my experience has brought
in humanity, otherwise seen as god
and the light I sustain leaves me flawed.

Tender my passions, let my progress be slow,
for the world I envision demands it so;
taught by my nerves, I welcome some power
and learn my technique from cloud and flower.

The elements roar in my outcast head
where reason and love would rule instead
but I share with my brother his lovelorn state
and would have it so at this early date.

*

130

To be born means to lie awake at night
torn by pride and the light rejects us.
We anger the angels within whose sight
the despoiled nature of our flesh reflects us.

We reprove one another for the eye not cleansed,
for the heart not watched, the mouth ill advised.
Around us lie friends with whose ways we dispensed
and their faces declare what our hearts surmised.

The peace we build may make us incline
to bold decisions and yet we despair
before simple love, enticed by the shine
of a suspect sun in the open air.

I hold my tongue and walk no more
until this darkness renders new
intentions with great plans in store
and even now I feel a few.

*

131

The temporary classification of felt love
makes no difference to those who espouse it.
If I were to plan my life rigorously
and kept records of each time you appeared,

would that fill in the abyss?

A question to be settled by experience.
I cradle my love against my breast
and carry its secrets about with me,
logically stimulated by political pressure groups

or cool around corners with criminals.

*

132

By perfection we mean love
in such a state that the noisome future
flits through chinks between the worn boards
twittering.

*

133

A length of rope or
a magnetic attraction fits
equally well where tissue negates itself

but the hind curses the evening air
as though lovely tear in maiden's eye
meant next to nothing here.

*

134

The good will of a thousand men
preaches against death by mortal attraction.
　The filling meal all artists feel
　when gazing where the mystic crown
　reflects the unstained light –
should not be wasted on our canine friends.

　I say: Be kind enough to dogs,
why not. Their intrepid leader hogs the spot.

*

135

Good fellow men, leave careful thought
for future offspring of the true spirit
on paper, wax or stone. But never

try it alone. Bring along others of a
kindred soul, whose genesis your will
respects and would not see maligned.

*

136

Naturally I am not ill at ease
about my salad says at home
where among goats, on rocky hillsides
I most eventfully did roam

never too much by myself to secure
a foothold on laughter's pitch
or tied to mother's apron strings
while my time grew rich.

'Do it yourself!' was my call
to the clouds reflecting shyly
the breaking-on-ardour's-rim
voice, and I heard it slyly.

Be a law to the sun's great
heat, and the earth, your bed
shall your nights winnow and weaken,
and bring peace to your head.

The cat chewed the snake to pieces
for me, that I would learn
how the mild moods of our life
protect us against love we earn.

*

137

So I am not the malingering
hero, his fire spent, haphazard on
borrowed wing, nor mechanical in my

flood-conquering assertions; or do you
doubt how far the willow sinks behind the
moon, or sits beneath the jackdaw?

*

138

So exactly you swerve to the right,
to the left, that the very issue from your mouth
troubles man's wisest. Yet we have begun
an immense finishing. Our lot

bears no tragic overtones. We
curb the massive tenderness in our soul
and reject the mean-eyed bear's heavy-handed
approach to a few slight problems.

*

139

What, you care for me
and still you prolong the agony of
a few days under Hyssop's spell?

*

140

I am intelligent enough to foresee:
    the thunder racks the cedar tree, though
formerly we kept ourselves apart and
    practiced the interlocutor's art.

*

141

    Why have we no other means
for tenderly espousing our own flesh
but only the abstract axe unseemly?

Why must our thoughts risk contumely,
handcuffed before the bar of jibe and jest?

Or should we crudely emphasize
the mystic flight-path parabolic?

    All my life I have limited my joys,
cropped the enervate longings for
high passion and success-mongering results.

    Now I bring my gladness down
to earth where politics run riot.

    I sit cross-legged in the market place,
shouldering the pleasure of my own proposals.

*

142

Deliver us into no stealthy hands.
I have innocuously begun my task
   and the drunken fools by the wayside

leap down from walls, taking no care.
They subject themselves to danger
   ordinarily allocated to fools.

Make permanent the truth's kingdom
within our eyes, that no miracle should
   be reaped where the elements last.

*

143

To match my eye   two moons required.
The unholy hour   has been desired.
All god's domain   by hate enmired.
The glory of deeds   drowned and fired.

*

144

Outside so much bears down on me,
the wicked wind, the half-slice of moon,
the swift unzipping the blue canopy,
that I measure myself by the truth.

And then the jewel of hedgerow green and white
perseveres with a life I would not have suspected.

Still I half fear the winter's desolation
and dream of double rainbows once or twice
arched over the New Town. Then ecstasy
unmans me for a period under the sun.

*

145

Talent watches how the pigeons wheel
showing dark backs, then underbellies bright,
then genius lifts this up against the white light
bridging horizons, fluttering in cool flame.

*

146

The poet paints still life if he must:
a street light rigid against the sky
as though blue cloud made war 'on line' –
still the emphasis of the thing remains.

*

147

Come out of your body and
thread the space needle of the flesh.

Cast aside systematic tremors,
you have schooled this all too frequently.

Clasp the quintessence of ether to your breast
and formulate posterity.

In the coolness of a late day's environment,
not yet prepared for the chance configuration
of the intruder, I fallibly link this and that,
murder, perhaps, and the sphere of birds,
conscious of my vocation but not dressed
for the work soon to exercise all my greatness.

And there I leave, lest a spell weave
too much of a troubled pattern here.

Halfway through a mood's deep anxiety
the bodily perversions steal off quietly.

Then, cruel mother, you may fill me with
gracious wonder, against all else.

*

148

The pockmarked face
casts its shadow
long among the trees
where spirit eddies,

strikes a crude pose
reminiscent of Hades,
then feels like ice
and glories in badness.

The vanquished rose
pretends to be ready
to bind and to loose,
to create new loads

as earth would rise
through our own rudeness,
given that we please
sweet lasses and laddies.

*

149

Happiness, jokes and joy
like a spring from me flow
and from every weakness my
laughter exploits a flaw.

My merriment no bounds knows
since this new light I see,
less contentious, easy ways
gladly to dispel, not rue.

In contradictions you smile
and on high ropes dance,
or point to a white sail
ever more cheerful since

my mirth broke from that
tree when lightning struck
my brain and moved it
to bring true bliss back.

*

150

My soul is clear,
my spirit not numb;
my mind reaches far,
my eye is not dim.

I speak what I mean
and declare my sense
wisely and right soon
while the light clean runs.

A most happy lot
is mine as I surmise,
and I would place a bet
that the world's ways

are all singled out
to please me dearly
or to see me right
when my flesh is poorly.

*

151

The mystic stream runs deep
    beneath stone
hewn from sound hope
    such as mine.

I have forgotten my anger
    several years
but lewd tastes still linger
    like cut flowers.

What I do must succeed
    and stand
whole, not on one side,
    merely found –

but the world always amuses
    as tricked stage
whose sacrificial smoke rises
    to some stooge.

*

152

As a sentenced criminal lies awake
in his cell to count remaining seconds,
his past sins his heart rebuke
in search of some enticing tokens
and though our faces may look alike,
our souls are of the same makings.

Outside his gate the dull watch sits,
secure to put his faith in locks
and steel chains; his hand pats
the strapping thigh, his mouth sucks
a wet cigar stub, then he trots
to stretch his legs while the clock ticks.

God's love shows many diverse states
to him whose eye remains unbroken,
though once our gaze views several lights,
pity and care are soon forsaken
and the hand whose fine skill most suits
the world's thirst is firmly shaken.

*

153

The foolishness in men drives
their hearts' contents to the brink.
The living light their eyes removes.

We have the pain in us to thank
for wisdom's unneglected fruit.
Challenge of self maintains the link.

Miracles press us with their might,
a thousand times the weight of gold.
Learn the signs of love by rote.

Those who once Caesar's office held
flee now before an unkind wind.
They shall not find this winter mild.

Oh teach the nature of mankind
and speak out plainly as you go.
See there the earth's king on his mound.

The heavens hold heir values high
while down there more than magic rules.
Our sexual essence wields its plough.

While intellect applies and files,
the costly will of man roves.
God's mercy from his hate recoils.

*

154

Today the sea enfolded
our senses as we walked
and its warm mists welded
our thoughts to what they liked.

The distant shores provided
moments of peace, provoked
by laughter, but not goaded.

The simple earth rested
beneath the sky and traded
its love, that none was wasted
and the sea heaved and sighed.

Some mindful gulls coasted
and a black shag mowed
the ocean's mass demurely.

With heavy hearts we paid
attention and left early
to avoid its private ailing
and we escaped it barely.

*

155

I keep my mind clear,
my tongue I discipline;
into the heart I call truth,
forth from the light I beckon it.

When my master calls
or I to him look for guidance,
the memory of my love rises
and of my conscience the satisfaction.

Therefore we rule our emotions
and wondrously we free them;
that you may accept,
we search out, this truth.

*

156

In the park the willows,
by the stream the beeches
tempt our annihilation,
conspire with our hopelessness.

Beyond, where the water rests
and the moon lies upon it,
we meet to have knowledge,
satisfaction of our desires.

In the coolness of the night,
as one who loves himself,
we return to our home,
to the kingdom we make our way.

*

KINA

Oh I want to lie down
        but my bed is soiled;
to the woods I would go to please me
        early, before light.

Why do my people despise me,
        their king and master;
they spit on my image
        provoked by their sin.

Only in heaven am I comforted,
        not on the street;
only in my works do I rest,
        not in captivity.

Rouse not my anger, Lord Jesus,
        against the vile ones;
my arm lift not up in violence
        over the heads of dogs.

*

158

My little table is laden
  with artefacts of language;
covered is the prop of my soul
  with an unwilling sadness.

My limbs ache from abuse
  my shoulder from a burden;
I tremble at the thought of intelligence,
  my feelings abhor me.

The work I have set myself escapes me,
  as cinders the fire's heat;
I am judged in my effort at love
  since ease is more becoming.

*

159

I fear I may say too much
and some would encourage the worm
to fly, the elephant to crawl,
so I shall contend myself with:

an illumination of the ear.

*

160

Is it by the ear I understand
or do some of these remarkable insights mean
that a blushing girl has given me the eye
and I have trouble behaving maturely?

*

161

The ear creates its inner space,
a room of resonance, open for inspection
but whatever you pick up or point out –
leave yourself an avenue of escape.

*

162

The understood space today
is small on purpose.
No more orchestration to disturb
the stars' fixed path is allowed.

We shall be free.

*

163

There is no more deplorable sight
than bluebells wilted and dried.

*

164

God did, as only god can,
drive me to the limits
to show there are no limits
except those god sets:

not pain and death,
for these, like world, are overcome
but the passions fulfilled and
justice satisfied to the overflowing.

*

Among a thousand hills lies
the mystery of the injured cloud

A day with light to spare,
and the courage to see it more
as living cloud on earth defiled,
to leave some heights unscaled –

a day such as my mother makes mourn,
my father makes yearn,
in his goodness unspeakable and fair,
but in my heart I care.

Look how the balanced trees survive,
or the rust on the boot-scrape beside the door;
look now the eye picks out at once
the white mysterious object insecure –

and fling forward into every street
the misery held back by the wall,
trampled underfoot by beauty's high heel,
beauty too harsh to feel.

Do not forget to look,
for the peace there in the grey mist
conjures with some primitive spite
and lays the ghost of an influential night.

The face of god sees me as I it
or looms with spectral inflammation
and the holy house held open for my despair
makes a nonsense of this fear.

*

166

These are weak days,
filled to the brim with frustration.
Nothing works twice.
I know nothing, except:

The discovery of my life depends on
how many miles I can travel before
the ruthless monster once more accosts me.

Do yourself some good: says my hand.
Hearken unto the being of sound: says
my ear, and demons scuttle for cover.

Eros breaches my senses' redoubt.
A fine maiden walks up the footpath
and god grants me the beauty of her sight.

This is not what the prophets expected
when they peered out time's window past
bricks and mortar into the rose's heart.

Leave me a shred of evidence, father,
that my life may continue to grow, not
heavily succumb to the death of the nations.

*

167

Let yourself dream a bit.
The nourishment of Christ's wine
oozes from the sandstone wall
or holds itself, like sunlight,
ready for the inspecting eye.

The clouds of sleep show mystic faces
in profile shadow against the washed wall.
Still I quake before the judgment's
refining mystery, catering to love.

*

168

On nature's trail, through government's maze,
by truth aroused, I shun inclement ways
and catch the last spark of solitude before
my spirit flags and I exist no more.

*

169

Lo, the pattern, the table supports
anxiety's sweaty restraint of horses.
I shall take my evening meal
and respect the universal forces.

*

170

Torture the heart only if it beheld
the promised lustre, tried and trusty.
Again search where night is rooted

and cling to generous will of god
settled before time's timorous trials
or look with scorn on the raven's retreat.

*

171

To another man my beguiling smile might
bring bewitchment and estrangement.
But for you this fostering light
means love's exquisite rearrangement.

*

172

The evening holds itself in peace.
Except for drums no warlike sound
sets starlings from the pine trees loose

nor interferes with my heart's wound
that heals and would not but for thee
whose words its pain in passion bind.

What power me from your world forth drew
insists now that my spirit weeps
and tears sheds wheresoever I go.

My heavy head in deep thought droops.
The torments, fears, embittered doubts,
the terror hot that sideways swipes

at easy life and all its rights,
with me here in daylight shall brood
until man's fate my sorrow sates.

Then I shall come out from my hide
so unobtrusive that no bird
or other wild thing by god made

finds its own kingdom's music marred –
then seek in vain in beauty's face
rude scars impressed there by time's sword.

*

173

Visions obscure my face.
The darker side of hills and trees
cuts heaven off, immerses
the sky in detrimental cloud.

Though who would force the night
from its conclave in the eye,
measure the output of black doubt,
assume the heart's accidental burden?

I would incinerate my life
and broadcast its remnants worldwide
but for the sense of your assurances,
the passion of intelligent amusement.

*

174

God's clay, my self, here to impress
his tender imprint, to show forth
what suits him, what suits me in turn,

his practice ground for untried games.

The hand that aids the unused child
guides me through wilderness of mind
and captivates the ill-willed brain,

dangerous beyond the bounds of man.

And where man's end is there god rests,
making him no unjust demands,
for man is god's whole interest true,

his one love, bound to him by Christ.

*

175

I am
not the sort of person I
like, but the sun shines on
me too, trouble me not.

My hair hangs down
deep into my image.

I loathe
the miasmatic credentials
of the butterfly.

Here, cook me a meal,
telephone an undertaker.
I'm a forlorn sod,
exactly as peaceful as
the loneliest man on earth.

*

176

1   Glory to the reborn man.

Do the stars not hold
enough attraction for his eyes?

Speak to him as though
his tired mind had left
no stone unturned for your welfare.

Then tolerate your heart
and give love sweetest
possible opportunity to
assail you and make you wise.

*

2   Exercise love's capacity.

To the god who made me I render
all due affection from a full heart.

What is man but god's most
ambitious project, lovely to behold,
capable of tender mercy in freedom.

Therefore I raise my voice in praise
and a clear spirit guides me through
thick and thin, never at a loss for
the creamy milk of human kindness

3   Urge the power of an almighty soul.

Why do hateful thoughts, set loose among
weak people, generate stupid strife?

I make no allowances for my own
future catastrophes, nor do I wish to
upset those who have others in charge.

It pleases the lords of life to
hang each other from abstracted branches
until rooks claw at the hollows of eyes
and the prayers of saints are inexpedient.

*

4   I am not alone here.

Vision remakes my world for me
and I invite my friends to join me.

Not that my cottage should stand
unassailed by water and wind
or the smoke from its chimney go straight.

If you care for the life we live,
why not step along this path and
accept the fruits of love, as they
tumble from the spirit's profusion.

*

5   I accept the discipline of my state.

For every happiness achieved there
a complex of guilt must haunt us.

So absorb the voices of contention
and forgive those who measure your worth
in accordance with the plague.

The love made by poets brings
peace over the land, and fruitful
awareness of all that pertains to the welfare
of men and women and their children.

*

6   Let me rest my abused flesh.

The wellspring of an effective reality
in the service of time awaits us.

Curb, therefore, the unborn appetites
and tremble before the world's fault
lest it fling our treasure under wheels.

I am no man's chattel, nor can I hope to
maintain my existence forever, but a breach
of trust signals a new work; why else
these stones weighing my heart down?

*

7   Love employs no other instrument.

It is you wanting to love or
being loved, adjusting the pain of it.

Let those praise you who must,
sing out never mind the ecstatic fling
nor the dredged mood, the scraped shell.

Utter the warning cry or hold your
tongue, as all men ought, and take
advantage of the earth's good things
but above all love continuously.

*

8   Our enemies alert us to love.

I specify: a contagious disease is called
mind; it creates false images.

Slowly perpetuate the skills required for
reality in practice – the enormous defeat
of a boastful heart, intent on rule.

Here too establish, once and for all,
outposts of mercy, bulwarks against
the lust for rapine, the heresy of deeds
unconfirmed, blind feeling of one's self.

*

9   Down comes justice in its own time.

Fear not, little ones, but oh you great
proud upholders of mighty rights: fear!

I am shamed to mention how often my
spirit painted itself for war against
curiosities and bludgeoned them to death.

Even yet I rear up in violence before
insults and compliments, or I bestow
a cheap thrill on unsuspecting ladies
when the mood takes me and shakes chaff out.

*

10   Better not to give than
to pretend to a largesse
where weeds choke fruit out.

I welcome the weight on my spirit
because I kill light-heartedly.

Oh odious refrain from day to day!

Now I wait, under the lamp, while
rain streams my eyes out, and off
red roofs harsh reflections split
nerves containing my youth.

*

11   What has entered my heart and
     arranges itself in comfort there
     as though this place belonged to him?

     Good! Appearances breathe again.

     I long for someone taking me down streets
     where doors stay open all night and
     the dog barks to confirm gratitude
     for services rendered, pains taken.

     But whether such a light shall burn
     in my lifetime I know not.

* * *

177

I would let my spirit lie on the meadow,
on green fields I would let it rest.
Where the hawk dreams above folding hills
my mind dreams too, over my failings,
and wheresoever I strive or stray
serious doubts dog my achievements.

Oh the impossible demands we make,
the outrageous claims, on god and one another,
the successes we fake, the wilful illusions
to fool death's eye, to render him tranquil,
when all time squats on carnal haunches
entertained by so much action for nothing.

Peace loses its seat in my body,
its throne it vacates, to limp among children,
with gypsies to roam, out of character.
My love sullies itself in the city,
on the gallows it searches for a lost immunity;
the tribes of the earth have nothing to offer.

I slide my hand in among the grasses
to pluck the poppy – and now I have it
firmly in my grasp – I eat the seeds.
Beneath my gaze multitudes destroy themselves
and I watch amazed, vaguely I observe,
as vision allies itself to its maker.

I have come to the end of my life on earth,
too tired to deal with the moods of mutants,
over-affected by poisons out of the sky,
by the taste of the succulent fruit called evil.
I shall lay me down on clouds of forgetfulness,
in mists of obscurity I shall lose my way.

There, in the jagged edge of the rose leaf,
unperturbed and just barely credible,
the wild juice sleeps, having found its limit,
while the powdery essence of the blossom rises.
Pigment and craft, spirit and makeshift
close mine eyes, my senses overshadow.

* *

178

The circle-round-the-island path,
the cries of sea birds in the air,
the tide arriving from far off
and high grass fragrant everywhere –

stones shimmering under water's film,
high clouds, warm sand, a small bird's nest
hidden behind the sandbank's screen
of sedge and reed, where eggs hatch best.

So many greens, the spirit fears
contamination from earth's dust,
but fields divide and hedges hide
and true love curbs the spirit's lust.

*

179

Give me a future, god of time,
for my eternity has run its wheel
into the earth down to the axle.

I cry for food from barns
empty since sunrise this day,
a forlorn creature, broken-mouthed.

I have lost the use of my eyes,
the mountains pile in on me,
I do not dare take my fate in hand.

Sickness and the expectation of pain
frighten me, make me cower behind
sheets of nausea, angry and rebellious.

My face sweats, the skin erupts,
I have become an abomination,
terrified by the pictures plaguing my mind.

God, test me no more, my intellect
craves death, a cold heart feeds on me
and I suspect no one cares how I fare.

Nevertheless I still learn, such as that
no one constrains your grace, and it might
suit me to bear this in mind as I pray.

*

180

Beauty is god's face, earth on fire
one day, the stars in cosmic trust
another, though how we use this power,
with half a heart, where we like it best,
or ground as heart's meal, to feed unliked
fitful children, who seem to have missed
the point of existence: this has provoked
some courtesy, some contempt, some bitter

regret, and the time's priests have rebuked
sacraments tied to the untried letter.
But man was never so sorely vexed.
We stand exposed to the tricks of matter
but feel, with a thirst for a life untaxed
by pain, its comfort, and oh, its sweet
promise of challenge with triumph mixed,

for our space is constrained, our time late,
and soon, we fear, we go to ground
and have not moved one single mote
in spite of sacrifice of mind,
nor have we sunk in god's mind lower
than our forbears, for whom mind reigned.

*

We reach beyond the dark caverns
scooped out by the Nile on its
allegorical descend. We ignore
the Welsh tribes failing in battle,
but our intellects cannot succeed while
love burrows secretly in trenches
maintaining itself for no reason.

Storms never feed on themselves long
but rage across unfixed dunes, hungry for
new sensation, the tribal past, excess
in terms of pine woods or pennies.

Look down between your feet, where
suddenly opens the uncharted abyss.
Let the stone fall noiselessly forever,
which means in an above average constancy
of hope now for the future eternal.

I am born to a task like most men, brothers.

I know what I want should happen
and some of this clings to the bark of trees,
tremendously fit for consumption, however
should the swoon ever lift off the earth
and hell be totally forgotten, not
teased in routine, I would merry be.

God gives me glimpses of what we must
pass through to get where we shall end up.

Therefore I say: Easy does it, yield
to forces that look as if they meant
to destroy, then let them overcome themselves.

*

182

The urgency to work,
to exemplify ourselves,
is respected at once
and we make ourselves responsible for it.

Now we wait, tools in hand, for material.

This process of waiting goes on indefinitely.

Any intellectual byplay is rejected, emotion
is absorbed. In this way the purity of the
heart, of the eventual operator, is
maintained.

The material substance arrives.

Preparation is over and work as such begins.

*

183

The cold, dry prison of the world
admits sunshine, reflects sunshine
back out. Birds alight on the wire
in a row. We wait to make our visit.

An anxious moment, when an inmate shouts,
passes. The gate opens and we enter.
Darkness overshadows our mind as we
walk along an empty corridor.

A figure in black wields keys
knowledgeably. Our expectations are
aroused. We hope not to be disappointed.
In the room stand a chair and a table.

Now we are on our own. Many years pass.
Our education takes its course. Death
has known others like us, who
broke down under similar circumstances.

Eventually the door opens again and
we are let out, respectfully, because
we have behaved ourselves. True,
one feels it may well have been worth it.

*

184

In easy succession the minutes fly,
the clock ticks; I wonder shall I ever
have final peace?

Oh never mind these strange thoughts about
how the day has gone, what mask it wore!
I am interested only in my dreams now
and if you come with me you may learn
where I spend the night.

Under this oak, its branches
touch the soil, we may be seated.
Here listen most carefully to the pale
darkness, imagine your absence,
become as still as your own womb.

The stars have much to celebrate tonight;
it seems, as though our presence here,
seen through the curtain of branches,
meant more to them than we recognize.

Oh mild climate, and the oak's trunk
in hard assurance against our back,
favourably disposed towards meditation,
and an illuminating spirit awakening within us.

The dancers do not obscure the actuality
of this place, nor have their cries
rent the stillness. Only their transmission
of gold from flesh to vision matters.

Take hold of these five token remembrances:
the sky at night behind eyesight, our own
misty declarations of love, the image of a
river, folded eyelids and an easy peace.

*

185

What a pity that you must die.
Could you not have held
on to your life while the roses
rushed to your aid and
brought their fragrance to bear on
what ails you, what fails you?

For these two, your chronic illness,
time's infatuation with itself, and
the illusion that you exist,
make an end of our association.

I dream of a freedom from you
where more happens than flight
and I may recall our friendship
with good conscience.

They celebrate your beauty
and your success with what you touch
while my own feeling is effaced,
lowered into deep forgetfulness.

Now who helps me cope with the snake
curling its thick body around
my throat of a summer evening
and who lifts the weight from my heart?

Go, spin yourself a cocoon of the
world and capture the gratitude
of those who stroll with hat and cane
down busy streets outside the park.

Be the 'other one', the one who
walks ahead, takes risks, shows
fits of temper for truth's sake
and pretends I have never lived.

*

186

While I search I make no mistake.

Beneath the forest floor roars
the earth, its waters call us.

An imaginary deer, stalked by
no hunter, pressed by its heart,
profoundly leaves the clearing.

I have drawn patience from such scenes
and the blood of Christ has flowed
through my veins while I held myself
ready for the final trial under the sun.

*

187

Go now and find perfection among the reeds.

A thousand stars have uplifted men's hearts
even while priests preached time's end.

A nettle plays host to the peacock's larvae
or washed flint drops from limestone walls;
therefore speak wisely in the presence of all.

Knowledge has a way of bearing forth truth
while nature's excitement trims man's mind
and casts in shadow predominant each bird's
rich harvest of earth's spellbound topography.

*

188

I shall not make my home again in notions.

The abstracted intensity of a child's eyes
haunts my pleasures as I rest beneath the yew tree.

The curse set upon the hill in stone and steel
makes rat traps for the villagers, or pours
contempt out on young heads, freezing them.

Surely we were born with senses to an end
and heaven's magnificence needs no explosives
tripped before a cat catches its mouse – one idea,
two thoughts, washed from the clever sea ashore.

*

189

Torment me not in mine eyes, oh love's plaything.

An immense obscurity hangs over the flushed houses
and much rain has cleansed their blind walls.

Lure vanity, four-legged temptress, from the city's
ashes and wait there, folding sheaves, straddling
emotions severally, as shame from the trees flocks.

An oak harbours a multitude of small things whose
world, riven by historic thunder, has overturned,
showing why love informs even the elements and
strikes no bargain for the sake of a full heart.

*

190

Don't be put off by rush hour traffic.

Those who neglect the hive's activity

must make plaint the gift of their being.
Gradually I incorporate the living breath,

worker of miracles, kept on ice
for the better part of twenty centuries.
And the welter of doubt, the morass of

suspicion, all ignorance for a day,
has to be scotched first, before I'll
trust my full weight to the last bridge.

*

191

Do not yield to the eye in the cloud
but achieve love's end here intact,
tempered by the burden, eyes wide,
hand easy, and let each joy depict
the realm of soul that will suit,
where once the child unmindful looked
and memory waved as from a height.

Rely on this and keep it firm:
love must step in where brain gives out.
Brain on its own will do us harm.
But love must not attach its eye
to any thing outside love's norm.
Love feeds on what love's senses know,
therefore remain within love's home.

If it should happen that I lose my way
or quarrel with the realm of time,
let me be burdened with what I feel,
that perhaps my pain may proclaim
the spirit's right to prosper or to revile,
the heart's choice to be kind or rude,
and yet not to make mockery of the rule.

*

192

I am not content with this life,
this eternal gestation of half-tried,
half-tested forecasts, blindly
adhered to by the physical self.

Therefore I unmask the things that
surround me, revealing their crass,
bunched phenomenality, seed in
speeding wind, form on fences.

According to love's logic one might
orchestrate one's inner self, make
melody with the outer, the perverse
make-shift thing, but to no avail.

So take care in future of the lone
world, not yet vended, but here
set up on plaster, there strung out
hopelessly between energy and sin.

*

193

Is this new world, then,
wholly a thing of fantasy,
god in my blood, and
should I not spurn it?

Paradise now turns out
a bitter pill to swallow.
I must learn, no help
for it, or create mischief.

Out goes another light,
darkness taking place,
moon faking more sense
upon the righteous sheet.

Leave me an illusion of
self-esteem to work with,
an invention perhaps to
trap mice in for food.

How horrible to share our
doubts with those who would
memorize faults, rather than
forgive and forget, father.

I am not given an image
to idealize, and those I
worked to that end plant
reality now by dying.

*

194

Oh Helen, dream come true for
a thousand souls prior to Christ,
I am nailed to the beam stretching
from the naked truth to particular
obscurity, and you aid me not.

Oh dear Beatrice, how did poor
Mrs. Dante feel, tell me, was she
of saintly understanding or did
the kitchen knife flash in her hand
when you beckoned him to the cloud?

Mary, you too have my eyes glazed
because you put up with society's
shocks, doubtless were told by some
that husbands mean trouble, or the
lack of one more, considering time.

And you too keep quiet, hold back
maybe, or should I in blindness
take the measure of my self-esteem,
asking: What would anyone have me
do, how behave, to live respectfully?

*

195

How comes this net of confusion over me?
I am not tormented, but rest sweetly
in a silence, before rejection upon a
heap of shame, stupidity and doubt.

I want to sleep, and wake up with
happiness dazzling me, naturally, or
did anyone suppose the life apostolic
precluded the ordinary hints of flesh?

No, even that leaves me dissatisfied, for
my loss stares me in the face, mirrored
there and there, preordained poses,
work as the basis for wine and roses.

How could I cope with the unfitting question,
with all the old alternatives trotted out
and me not built for dealing with people,
only steadfast song, love in the twilight!

Jesus, my lusts leave me hankering for
the quiet, reasonable life, but no person
is left for me to challenge while sea wind
blows salt weed fragrance across to me.

*

196

Teach this poor sod to distinguish.
I am alone in my predicament,
the people live to entertain and
where I look my blood flows.

These are wise decisions, made under
duress, to no pretty tune, flattering
the priest's greed at the door, pampering
god's children to please horses.

Nor do my lips exalt vainly great
monuments, left to bleach on
female hills, organized by rote,
but I look into your finished eyes.

One moment leaves me well altered,
then the reasoned heart strikes,
the terror from scarcity of food,
lately imagined as a deliverance.

But while my prayer functions
I pick fruit delightfully hanging
into the sober, clear spirit; wish
only to be like you, waiting here.

*

197

I have absorbed so much
sun and rock and sea, merging
the presence of love with its earth-
spell, that the questions you ask

come to me like the tern's flight,
whipping with thin scissor shapes
the pellucid air, each rising a gift,
    or they operate aerobatically.

Do you tone down for me, god,
this vast sweep of expansive dream,
settling rocky outcrop here, cushions
of herb, thyme, thrift and trefoil

there, and the swallows skipping
perhaps over dewy grass, so that
elegance may the beflecked flesh breach
    and work beauty's separation?

For the holy cosmos must stand
alone, beyond atonement and
reparation; should ever sanctify
life's attributes, nowhere as near as

now in what we call heart's existence,
mind's being, rooted as brain-cell:
fear gives no quarter once you flee
    before the tide's winnowing.

*

The Copelands

Patches of god's presence some times
illuminate the place where I stand
and I know I am here to be guiled
by trappings to hold me now fast.

Willow herb, I remember, in unison
confined the breathing flesh of god for me
where since the spade has torn earth up,
and this was meant as a comfort.

*

The island where overhead the gulls rage,
belabouring the intruder with ridicule,
and the step sags into soft turf,
takes me to task for my formality.

Here a few houses dot the landscape,
sheep's wool hangs from bracken fronds
in waxy handfuls, and the dull sea
lies there waiting, an immense anomaly.

The boat ties up, avoids the stone's edge
and below the seaweed slaps in clusters
against the exposed sea bed; or sails
loom suddenly around the spit.

Emphasize the entire mind's view of it.
These visions had, as it were, escaped
at the time, or lain in wait elsewhere,
or gone to ground, in perfect harmony.

So naturally I express my gratitude
knowing that others feasted here too
but have not the gift of eternal digestion,
bringing me gladly into man's community.

Fond thought? Never you mind the leer
of the dead friend, the haphazard stranger
whose mask reveres all obscure ghosts.
I have no one in particular in mind.

Perhaps I should, who knows; earlier
these trembling attitudes, emotions pure,
purely and simply contacted sensitivity,
contracted the eye in a spineless squint.

Now I point to the rage within and say:
The gulls circle, let the gulls roam,
let their fine skulls bleach another year
on the sand, among nettles and bugloss.

Protected from mere exercise in profusion
by healed wounds once speared by the
artistic intellect, one contemplates
removing a dead gull's head to boil it.

Would that not show how perfectly bone sits?
The feathery bag lies flung into the gravel.
The dejected head roars and ridicules
no more, but serves to expose my weakness.

Then all goes blank, probably because
I am not meant to make too much of
god's true greatness, man's flaws,
and the dried seaweed crunches underfoot.

With each step more darkness leaps up
to consume a fear, to blot a doubt
where no such thing ought to hinder
the simple blue sky's cheerful smile.

From afar off the island's outline seems
a trick, as the white water washes
succeeding waves, rolling away a while,
then steaming into mists of rationality.

* *

Dear parent, creator of all this universe
in a justice that makes my heart's eye fill,
makes me feel benefit for having been born,
bearing a day with a lesser justice:

do not look out unkindly on what drifts
in amused wonder past these gunwales,
for I detect a fitting here for oarlocks
and the skipper's eye is trained for remedy.

* * *

Captivity in the Nature of Things

Captivity lies in the nature of many things.
The hot air rises up out of a meadow
where a donkey is tied, munching buttercups.

We expect too much, we achieve too soon
when all space out there means our living room
or fervour whips us to lay down disguises.

You may have marched across an open field
intent on giving better than you were given
when a beetle's progress there on the chervil's

white head, steeped in fragrance, bids you
hesitate, to accumulate a moment's flow,
to take life's mirrored image nice and slow.

Then you may see the horses, patiently fenced,
or a duck and drake meshed in eager flight.
It pleases you to stand, to stare and wonder.

Beneath, the soil's mute constancy exists,
or the veiled roots of pine and hemlock drive
a steady bargain with the season's riches.

Do likewise, son of man, stand not on ceremony
or fidget with a raised brow's dim excuse
while earth and sky brood in majestic harmony.

Leave off exploiting love's adroit intimacy,
for the sea swells and ebbs anew each day,
teaches sojourn, rough justice against rock,

blocks off all chance of rot and mildew
by bathing eyes and feet of us in salt,
which we may come to recognize, unappalled.

Rise, head! Balance on shoulders, keep
changing gravity's rationale into spirit's
substance for taste and sight, into love's

attentive touch, the untempting burden assumed,
the step taken into no flash of murk and mud,
the sign adopted for the sake of tall children.

Even the attitude we take towards thought
can box the landscape in, paint an estate
in lurid hues, who knows to what extent

festive and how far suspicion has crept in
and chained the old Alsatian to the gate
to pace on leaf-mould while the flies gather.

Castles still perch on hills and reminisce
of times when sheer weight left its mark on conscience,
and earls rest beside dukes beneath black slabs.

Outside the gardens swell with considered pride
in rhododendron, holm oak, larch and yew,
not to mention the fine limbs of Scots pine.

That's how we thought in those days when we planted
and our inner life sought external exultation
where death was sure, a certain end to things.

Now we break out of these fetters and we escape,
on one hand into empty calculation, breathing
no air and provoking an absent god no more,

and into a new love on the other, where relations
with people, god and things still need establishing –
but never mind, it comes without our doing.

Effort in man therefore is a rare thing, required
to keep love in touch, no, nothing spectacular
like that hateful thirst for triumph over triumph.

Effort is captive if it holds in love, waiting
as much as striving, knowledgeable within
bonds, with a taste for suffering setbacks.

It only takes a finger to blow up cathedrals,
and battleships burn due to one man's fancy.
Robots build dams, fling bridges across chasms

with ease, produce butter mountains, milk lakes
at the flick of a switch, not gullible or naïve
like some, but with intentions of high purpose.

I can sit on my love's bed stroking her downy
back while telephoning for a tray of snails and
by the way create jobs for a million machines.

But then that's my lot, and I say so wisely
not mindless of another man's truthful mansion
or of my own greed, momentarily asleep.

I freeze or flame, perched on three-legged discipline
voluntarily exposed to the poisoning times,
making sense of faulty flesh cropping within.

I am not he whom you see walking to town
to purchase ink, and a fish , and a brown loaf,
or then he also, pressed into service from a sphere

where matter flows abundantly, infinitely here
to be used and used up, vexatious in relation
as we loaf, yes, even evil unless we live,

and the vision I have of happiness espouses all,
god, grain and gadfly, gives to all its due,
leaves none who has to struggle to be loved.

*

And yet I am dissatisfied with my deeds
and no one so far mentions them and says:
Yes, more of that, please, and make it wholesome.

* * *

200

Fear and Love

Fear rises and springs.
It tears up many things
and scatters their shreds.

We must make fear cringe,
not those it flays.
Then true love stays.

*

201

When you are old and know that fear
springs out at things and eats the heart's temper
and have made a habit of your father's remembered care

will these suspicions of deficiency seem silly
or will more achievement always breed more strife
and the lesson learned end in more risks taken?

*

202

Master me, Jesus, as I would mastered be
and safeguard my intentions from overweening.
Mother me, Mary, that my heart finds rest
and sinks into oblivion to renew itself.

*

203

Lady, you have my welfare at heart.

In the garden you speak on my behalf
and the messages from your mouth conquer evil.

I am not content to imitate the stars
nor will my trouble cease this year
unless the perfection of your rose aids me.

An enchantress once played you on the stage
and the world grew fond of all its glory,
neglecting the Olympians dressed in white,
frowning upon the heart's limited prescriptions.

We encase ourselves now in iron and steel,
meekness rides at the very end of the procession,
and while darkness threatens the dreams of children,
coercing the moon where no new blood flows,
my righteous thirst sees you as a consequence.

*

204

Cool, the breeze blows, perhaps
my perdition, as on horseback these
four gentlemen express their natures,

and don't you effortlessly assume
perfection as an exquisite thing
rather than a million attentions?

Bow out of some contests if
moods play an excitable role
or fellow travellers make love.

By the next ship we sail
forth from these island shores
into arms not yet practiced.

*

205

God sets store by manners mild
yet once did a violent gesture upheave
all that world stood for, making level

an Egyptian institution, crowned kings,
and the pattern of succeeding days was set.

We compared haloes, dusted shoes,
fenced off forgotten territories there

and while the life around us egged us on
to higher things, more money, less fortune,
God knew that you and I loved one another.

*

206

I am no example to my forebears,
nor do the coming years degrade me now
and while the jack-of-all-trades squats on love,
righting the wrongs of civilized endeavour,
I bide my time, and hide behind these things.

The mind, purposed to a mental energy
or fully fashioned, fledged out to some struggle,
can do itself no injury, but may reckon
on the world's aid; may satisfy itself
in logical pursuit, as flesh and blood.

*

207

Knowing that being has been finished
helps me finish mine
and since my roots reach down into the truth
what pleasure to do work out here –

where the sun sheds its light
and minstrels gladly know of one another
even if our laughter at times submits
to a crooked grin, in love corrected.

*

208

Come, heart, put aside this jubilation,
for know you not, the life you find
pivots itself on suffering men's bones?

*

209

Speak to the world in ways
easy to recognize
and bring down upon the heads
of happy and sad folk alike
no awkward illuminations
but the quicksilver stream of love.

*

210

I am conscious of a prepared love
as easy to recognize as the wood
and in its ease spirits sit there
mindful of each other's passion,

or a queen rises each morning
before dawn touches her brow
and chided, she flees,
waking all men in her path.

*

211

Go and tell the wildflowers standing
knee deep in the meadow's grass
of the path your fancy's taken
or, before the birds awaken
find them, dreaming, in your
        looking glass.

Light your love a candle.
Speak softly, that she might hear.
Oh, she kneels before the sun's
exquisite music as it runs
in her ear, sweetly
        in her ear.

Form a passionate attraction
for the world's intemperate wiles.
Bring your heart to bear on tuning
untried strings and, without swooning
stand by while the god you
        know smiles.

*

212

Project outward towards the world's darkness
the limited light invested within you
and keep your back turned, for the whole light
knows no before or afterwards; no training
of the imagination makes this light whole.

But the cold light feeds upon your soul's negativity
and you must penetrate where clouds have moved
so that nothing may alter your state of being
nor should it occur to anyone watching
that the light you spend has cost you anything.

Do you know where the day's living heart beats
and how the stag mounts to the upper part of the woods,
intent on trial and to will its foundation?
Can anyone sharpen the edge of experience for you,
too near to be equated with bliss or harm?

I am eager to join those who sing songs,
who praise god to please him, for no other reason,
and the ashen face of many a bystander
perpetuates in gesture, saga and legend –
but oh, the foolishness of an unquiet heart!

*

Index of first lines

Index of first lines in alphabetic order

* * * * *

* * *

*